STORIA 5
A WOMAN'S EYE VIEW OF BRITAIN TODAY

STORIA 5

A WOMAN'S – EYE VIEW OF BRITAIN TODAY

PANDORA

LONDON SYDNEY WELLINGTON

First published by Pandora Press, an imprint of the Trade Division of Unwin Hyman Limited, in 1990.

PANDORA PRESS
Unwin Hyman Limited
15/17 Broadwick Street
London W1V 1FP

Allen & Unwin Australia Pty Ltd
8 Napier Street, North Sydney, NSW 2060, Australia

Allen & Unwin New Zealand Pty Ltd with the Port Nicholson Press
Compusales Building, 75 Ghuznee Street, Wellington, New Zealand

---

British Library Cataloguing in Publication Data

Storia. – V –
1. Short stories in English. Women writers,
1945 – Anthologies
823'.01'089287 [FS]

ISBN 0-04-440695-9

Phototypeset in 12 on 14 point Bembo by
Input Typesetting Ltd, London
and printed in Finland by Werner Soderström Oy

If you were expecting fiction in this edition of *Storia*, then I hope that you will not be too disappointed to discover that it is fact – funny, disturbing, provocative and interesting articles about the state of Britain today. Once in a while, every healthy magazine produces a special that fits the time.

Angela Phillips looks forward a decade to consider how workplace nurseries, which are so ardently advocated as an aid for working mothers, might become tyrannical in their hold over women, Lucy O'Brien traces the growth of pop music in an effort to explain the current trend in revivals and Dyan Sheldon is just plain funny. Eva Figes criticises the new conservative 'Bingo' society where every player cannot possibly be a winner, and in two articles by Ruth Richardson we are reminded of the need to preserve our heritage for the future, learn from it and above all enjoy it. Jennifer Potter spent twenty-four hours in a lunatic asylum which is soon to be closed down as part of the government's 'care in the community' policy, and Michelene Wandor considers the particularly British habit of separating amateurism from professionalism.

We have also asked foreign journalists whose job it is to report on Britain for their readers back home how they see us. Their answers are, not surprisingly, less than flattering. Finally, a charming piece of razor-sharp satire on the conventional school essay from Natasha Vitaliev, written during her first visit to Britain from the Soviet Union, puts us firmly in our place, reminding us of our privileges as she highlights particularly humorous aspects of the British Character. I sincerely hope that nobody will be offended.

Kate Figes
Editor

CONTENTS

With photographs by Anita Corbin

NOTES ON CONTRIBUTORS

Dyan Sheldon was born in the USA and now lives in London. Her published novels are *Victim of Love* (1982) and *Average Man* (1985).

Ruth Richardson is the author of *Death, Dissection and the Destitute* (1988). She works at the Institute of Historical Research at the University of London.

Anne Cendre has been a correspondent for the *Tribune de Genève* for the past fifteen years.

Eva Figes is the author of eleven novels and *Patriarchal Attitudes*, a seminal work of feminist social criticism.

Melissa Benn is a journalist and writer. Her book *Death in the City* was published in 1986.

Michelene Wandor is a poet, playwright and critic as well as a writer of prose fiction.

Mary Stott has been a journalist throughout her working life, most notably as the creator of the *Guardian* Women's Page.

Lucy O'Brien is the author of a biography of Dusty Spring-field and a forthcoming biography on Annie Lennox. She is also a journalist writing for the *Guardian*, *NME* and *Elle* magazine.

Angela Phillips is a journalist and writer. She is the co-editor of the UK edition of *Our Bodies Ourselves* and the author of two books on pregnancy and childcare published by Pandora Press.

Jennifer Potter has published two novels, *The Taking of Agnes* and *The Long Lost Journey*. She is currently working on a horror story set in Czechoslovakia.

Sheila McKechnie is the director of the charity and pressure group Shelter.

Virginia Ironside is a writer, journalist and Agony Aunt for the *Sunday Mirror*.

Natasha Vitaliev trained as a chemical engineer and has worked as a guide at the permanent exhibition of Scientific and Technological Achievements in Moscow. She is married to the journalist Vitaly Vitaliev.

One World

DYAN SHELDON

'But they don't have cars like we do, do they?' said my
mother, her voice echoing through space.

I said, 'What? Mom? What are you talking about, Mom,
"they don't have cars?" Of course the British have cars.
Haven't you ever heard of the Rolls-Royce?'

Cables groaned, the satellite bleeped, and somewhere in
Georgia a woman asked her husband to bring her back
marmalade. 'You know, honey,' the woman was saying on
what seemed to be a far clearer line than the one connecting
my mother and me, 'that real old English marmalade like
Marsha Wynette brought back from London. It was so
delicious. You can't get anything like it over here.'

But my mother had moved on from automobiles. 'And
what about the toilets?' she wanted to know. 'Mrs Lovell
at the church said they've still got outhouses there, even in
the city. Isn't that something? Outhouses in the city?'

My sigh was lost in the echo, the bleep, a rusty sort of
rattling sound, and something more about marmalade that
I couldn't quite catch. 'Mom,' I said, 'Mrs Lovell at the
church was in England during the war, for Pete's sake. She
spent most of the time in a tube station. And anyway, things
have changed, you know. The toilets aren't outside any

more. We've got indoor plumbing. Most houses even have electricity. Any day now we're getting television.'

'But they don't have heat, do they?' said my mother. 'Do you remember when Mrs Andreas had that Englishman staying with her and he was always complaining that it was too hot? Three feet of snow outside and he was sleeping by an open window. It practically drove her nuts. That and him always leaving the bread out of the ice box. "You Americans," he was always telling her, "you keep every-thing in the refrigerator." And he just refused to watch television. Just point-blank refused, thought it was all junk. Even *Bilko*. I don't think they know anything about hygiene, if you ask me.' There was another crack, echo, rattle and hum. And then, 'Maybe I better bring my winter coat,' said my mother.

'Mom,' I said, 'I know London's three thousand miles from Brooklyn, but surprisingly enough it's May here too. I think you can risk leaving your winter coat at home.'

'What about food?' asked my mother. 'Should I bring some food with me? I bet they don't have Lipton's tea there, do they? I only drink Lipton's tea. Not because it's American, but because it's the best. And Mrs Lovell says it's very difficult to get fresh fruit.'

'Mom, please, you're coming to London, not trekking through Kathmandu.'

'At least the weather would be better in Kathmandu,' said my mother. 'Don't think I don't know all about the rain.' Linked by satellite and I could still see her purse her lips. 'Mrs Lovell told me.'

And my mother, of course, as she often is, was right. On the whole, the weather is better in Kathmandu than it is in the British Isles. In fact, I think it's pretty safe to say that

2

in the history of the world there has never been one single American who, sitting in her back yard in Southern California, sipping a piña colada while the hamburgers sizzled on the grill and the flowers seemed to glow in the evening light, has suddenly turned to her spouse and said, 'Hey, Harry, I've got a really great idea! Why don't we go over to London for a while? I hear it's really cold and dank there this time of year. I hear that no one in England has ever managed to have a barbecue when they weren't dressed in their ski parkas and galoshes and standing over the fire with an umbrella. Can you imagine? What a hoot! It might even be a good opportunity to pick up a chest infection or a little arthritis.' And never in the history of the world has Harry then met the twinkling eyes of his soul's mate, his own eyes glittering with excitement, and shouted, 'Honeybabe, now I know why I love you. You are an absolute genius! What an experience this will be. Did you know that the English still use hot-water bottles? We could bring back a bunch and give them to our friends for Christmas. Won't they get a kick out of that?'

Hot *what*?

Americans come to Britain because it is still, for many of us, the Motherland. Britain gave us our language, many of our ideas on government, human rights and sex, many of our ideas of literature and culture, our founding fathers and our first presidents, and mercifully few of our ideas on cooking. Americans come to Britain because their grand-parents came from Glasgow, or their great-grandparents were starved out of Ireland, or their mother's mother was born in Chiswick. They come here because they recognise the place names and can read the menus. Because everything is both foreign and familiar.

Americans love England because it is so quaint and charming: so old. Coming from a country whose history, so far as most of us are concerned, ends abruptly in 1492 – a country where anything over a hundred is ancient, a country that, in effect, is to the planet what Milton Keynes is to England, a new town that doubles as a shopping centre, and which, for the most part, confines the historic to its theme parks – they can't get over the fact that Britain's past is so visible, so close at hand. You walk through London, for instance, and every road and every alleyway holds secrets. Every church and every row of shops and houses tells a story. Here is the place where kings cavorted, there is the spot where famous poets collapsed in drunken heaps; here the meeting place of conspirators or painters, there the spot where the mistresses of ministers or the children of merchants strolled in the sun; here and there and everywhere the taverns visited by queens, composers, pirates, artisans, highwaymen and philosophers, the shops frequented by courtesans and architects, the houses lived in by Dickens. It is not like that in America. America started yesterday. America does not build on but over. There are no medieval ruins in New Jersey. There are no 700-year-old castles in Nebraska. Maryland has a sad lack of Tudor cottages and cobbled courtyards. In America, the old houses are leisure centres, our historic churches and farms and landmarks are drive-ins and parking lots and fast-food chains, and even our sacred Indian burial grounds are all under housing developments and shopping malls.

Americans often choose to stay in Britain because they feel it is a more gentle, more civilised place to live. Not crass and commercial, tough and aggressive like where they come from. The British, after all, are a race of gentlemen with stiff upper lips and a great sense of humour. They are decent and honourable, they have traditions and values.

4

Theirs is an older world, both more cultured and more staid Most of the Americans I know who live permanently in London, left home for a single, clear, uncluttered reason: they wanted to get away from Florida or Pennsylvania or Texas or Minnesota. Most of them have chosen to stay in Britain for an equally clear and simple reason: it isn't America.

'I still think you should've let me buy some bananas,' said my mother, settling into the corner booth of the restaurant near the fountain. Music that was neither one thing nor another played softly in the background. Tired of being wet all the time, I'd finally taken my mother to Brent Cross for the day. Thousands of miles across the raging, mythic ocean in order to go to a shopping centre.

'Mom,' I said, not as patiently as I had the first few dozen times I'd said this, 'Mom, you've got to stop trying to buy bananas. You've got to try to understand: there is no longer a fruit shortage in Great Britain. That was during the war. Now you can buy bananas whenever you want. You can buy mangoes and ugli fruit and papaya. We are no longer restricted to root vegetables.'

My mother shook her head, looking around her sourly. For the first time it struck me that in her beige all-weather coat, her headscarf and her sensible shoes, she could pass for one of those Englishwomen of a certain age who travel everywhere in twos, shaking their heads and worrying about the young. All she needed was a string bag or a basket on wheels.

'Look over there,' said my mother. 'Are those Puerto Ricans?' Two handsome young men in track-suit bottoms and heavy metal T-shirts, multicoloured basketball boots on their feet, leather bracelets and silver bangles on their wrists,

5

skeletons dangling from their ears, and their pitch-black hair pulled back in ponytails by neon-pink elastics, were sitting a few tables away.

'They're not Puerto Rican.'

'They look Puerto Rican.'

'Mom, we're in London, England, home of Winston Churchill, William Shakespeare, Barbara Cartland and the Queen, not the Lower East Side. Those guys are not Puerto Rican.'

'They're eating chocolate chip cookies,' noted my mother.

'They're drinking milk shakes.'

'Give me a break, will you, Mom? You eat pizza and you're not Italian.'

'That's not the same thing and you know it.' My mother shook her head again, this time almost sadly. 'I don't know,' said my mother. 'England isn't exactly like I pictured it.'

'Britain,' I corrected.

'Maybe I should've come in the winter, when it doesn't rain so much.'

I picked up my menu. 'It always rains so much,' I said shortly. The special of the day was a croissant filled with chilli con carne.

My mother and I had been seeing the sights for nearly two weeks. We'd discovered an above-average Mexican restaurant in Edinburgh. We'd discovered Dallas Cowboys shirts in Bristol and Jack Daniels beach towels in Camden. We'd discovered that the shortbread my mother usually bought in Brooklyn was both cheaper and better than the shortbread she bought on the Mull of Kintyre. And I'd discovered that my mother was not the perfect, good-natured, amenable American tourist I had become accustomed to over the years – the tourist you see docilely queuing up in front of Madame Tussaud's in the rain or buying

tartan blankets on the shore of Loch Ness. My mother did
nothing but grumble and complain. 'There's a Madame
Tussaud's near your Aunt Carmela's in Tampa,' said my
mother. 'I bought a tartan blanket in Macy's.'

For although my mother, like most of us, is happiest
when surrounded by things that she knows, she is also one
of those people who think that if you go to a foreign country
you should be struck more by the differences than the similarities. My mother, for example, had been impressed by
the palace, but disappointed to see not princes and princesses
and horse-drawn coaches 'like at the wedding', but streets
filled with people all dressed in such similar track suits
and trainers that, except perhaps for the Japanese, it was
impossible to separate the visitors from the natives. She
hadn't expected Hyde Park to be so similar to Prospect Park.
She'd been very surprised not only at the amount of traffic,
but at the size of the cars. 'Fords?' my mother kept saying.
'BMWs? Suzuki jeeps? Whoever thought you'd see a Suzuki
jeep in London?' Advised by her friends who had been on
the Senior Citizens' trip to Britain a few years before never
to get in a cab that wasn't black, she'd been a bit put out
to learn that so few of them were black any more. 'But it
looks like a newspaper,' grumbled my mother the first time
I shoved her into one. 'Why would they want it to look like
a newspaper?' She didn't understand why she couldn't get
an English muffin in England. She was openly distraught
that having been warned by Mrs Lovell that beer in Britain
was always served warm, like blood – a thought that had
struck horror into her heart back in Bensonhurst, 'Can you
believe it? *warm* beer?' – the beer in the first pub I took her
to was not only cold but American. 'What's this?' grumbled
my mother. 'Budweiser? Michelob?' She shook a bag of
taco chips in my face. 'Dos Equis?!' roared my mother. 'Is

that English? With *lime*? How can they have limes when they don't have bananas?'

My mother was equally distraught that, having been told at great length by Mrs Lovell about the British cinema – old music-halls badly converted into movie houses, hard seats, smoking sections, four hours of advertisements before the feature, chocolates and sweet popcorn ('Sweet popcorn,' my mother had said brightly as we started out to see a film, 'can you beat that? Who but the English would think of eating sweet popcorn? You think that's something from the war, or what?') – she had found herself in an eight-screen complex that sold Baskin and Robbins ice-cream and nacho chips with spicy cheese sauce. My mother did not want Baskin and Robbins ice-cream and nachos with spicy cheese sauce and an ultra-modern eight-screen complex, things she can get at home. She longed for the foreign. She craved the exotic. And the exotic to her was not tepid tea and a dried scone in The Sherlock Holmes cafe. My mother wanted hansom cabs and fog. She wanted the brave, stubborn, suspicious and slightly eccentric people of Mrs Lovell's stories and 1950s British comedies. She did not want to trudge around London from one blue plaque to another, dodging skateboards and pizza delivery bikes and tough teenagers in baseball caps and Walkmen, trying to imagine this building when it wasn't law offices on top and a wine bar underneath but the home of a famous statesman; trying to imagine that Thai restaurant when Mozart stayed there; trying to picture Thomas Hardy's house when there wasn't a minicab office next door; trying to visualise the island where the Brownings once picnicked on soft summer days when it wasn't under the flyover.

My mother wanted to see the *real* England. In the *real* England, you ate steak and kidney pie and Yorkshire pud-

8

ding, not hamburgers and chicken burritos. In the *real* England, everyone in Oxford rode around on bicycles; you couldn't order a pizza over the telephone; the streets weren't filled with kamikaze motor-cycle messengers; the call boxes were red and enclosed, not designed to look like space modules; the little boys wore short pants and blazers, not surfers and bright-coloured sweatshirts; the young girls were sweet and demure with peaches-and-cream complexions, not brash and loud and made up just like the girls back home. My mother wanted to return to Brooklyn with stories of old-fashioned tube trains and buses and phone boxes. Of bobbies on bicycles and rosy-cheeked children so much more polite and better educated than the children at home. Unfamiliar food. Unfamiliar clothes. An unfamiliar way of life. She didn't want to go back to Mrs Lovell and say, 'Hey, guess what? They've got Dunkin' Donuts and Taco Bell in Piccadilly Circus now.' She wanted to go back to Mrs Lovell and say, 'You were right, Dorothy, if I'd brought a bunch of bananas with me I could've made a fortune.' She didn't want to go back to Mrs Andreas and have to confess that the British now had central heating and double glazing, that it was now possible to sit in the home of an Englishman without your coat and gloves on. That they all had fridge-freezer combinations and kept their bread on the bottom shelf, next to the beer. She didn't want to mention the *Bilko* reruns. Kent had reminded my mother of Connecticut. Scotland had reminded her of Maine. Her only comment on Stonehenge was that it looked a lot like Wisconsin.

'I mean at Christmas,' said my mother. 'When it snows all the time. I've always liked carols, you know.'

Besides the chilli con carne croissant, the restaurant offered pitta bread with a choice of fillings, stuffed baguettes, lasagne, pizza, hamburgers, baked potatoes, hot

9

dogs, and pastrami on rye. 'It never snows in London,' I snapped.

'Don't tell me it never snows in London,' my mother snapped back. 'I've seen *Scrooge*.'

What my mother should have done, of course, was visit me when I arrived in London in 1977, long before Mrs Thatcher, clamouring for a return to Victorian values but striding forward into the brave new world of twentieth-century consumer capitalism, changed Britain once and for all. That first year, I lived in a squat, with no heat, no hot water, a toilet out behind the wash house (which still, amazingly enough, had its copper kettle), and plastic sheeting in the windows instead of glass. The following year I lived in a council towerblock, still with no heat but with hot water and an indoor loo.

In those days, it was still not uncommon for people not to be on the phone or not to own a car. In those days, I knew no one who had a shower, central heating or a Magimix. It was difficult to get avocados, pumpkins, cold beer, grape juice, or rye bread. I spent two years dreaming of pastrami sandwiches and falafels, missing *M*★*A*★*S*★*H*, longing to be able to take off my shoes and sweater in the house. The first McDonalds had just opened on the Edgware Road (the clue, perhaps, to the new direction), but aside from that everything was different – the fashions, the food, the television, the newspapers, the books, the music, the attitude to life. Everything was British. And British was still, well, old – old-fashioned – and very, very British. Despite the swinging sixties, there was still an atmosphere of mucking through and making do. Of restraint, deprivation and hard times. It was not a nation of luxuries or of self-indulgence. Not a nation of flamboyance. It was a brave, proud, stubborn, suspicious and slightly eccentric nation, still totally itself.

And it certainly wasn't difficult to imagine the past in 1977, because the past – at least the immediate past of the last thirty or forty years – was still very much with us. Gas fires and paraffin heaters. I'd lived with pot-belly stoves in the wilds of Upstate New York, but paraffin heaters in the capital city – the paraffin man calling in the street on Tuesdays and Fridays, the blue plastic container, the smell, the danger – were something else again. Shopping in the market. No ultra-modern supermarkets with thirty-one electronic tills, olive purée, balsamic vinegar and Senegalese dwarf green beans. No, not in 1977. Cabbages, potatoes, sprouts and salad cream. No one in London had ever heard of a taco. I had to have my herbal teas and my jelly beans imported. No one in London would have been caught dead walking down the street with head-sets on, listening to some young black man sing about sex. London was rain and drizzle, damp and grey. London did not have street life; the streets in London were used simply to get you from one place to another, bundled in your dark coat and muffler, eyes down and footsteps quick. London was unheated houses, metered electricity, and buses it was easy to fall off that stopped running at eleven o'clock. London was Wimpy bars (frequented, it seemed, because they were acknowledged to be so bad), the only Chinese take-aways in the universe that sold chips, and the one-limp-leaf-of-lettuce salad. Flannel sheets, a sight not seen in Manhattan for quite some time (if ever), were easy to come by, but not cotton ones of bright, bold colours, not ones of interesting or amusing patterns. Little girls still wore long white socks and patent leather shoes. It was possible to buy a pair of basketball

11

boots, but not easy to buy them – and you certainly never saw anyone else wearing them. People still called me a Yank. 'You a Yank, then?' they'd ask. I felt as though I'd been beamed into a British black and white movie, *circa* 1953. I couldn't believe that the city I'd come to and the city I'd come from existed on the same planet.

Now, as my mother found out, they not only exist on the same planet, they are rubbing up against each other in a quite alarming way. Now transatlantic-looking men talk on portaphones in restaurants that serve spinach salads and enchiladas. Now answer-machines and patterned tights and fudge brownies are commonplace. Times have changed indeed when you can buy Haagen Dazs ice-cream in Sainsbury's. Times have not merely changed but transmutated when you can walk through London and imagine that you are not in Britain at all but in a Coca-Cola commercial. All of a sudden everyone is wearing luminous sportswear and baseball caps. Boys with East-End or north-London accents look as though they come from Jersey or Philly. Cheryl and Samantha from Willesden might have just arrived from the suburbs of Minneapolis. Suddenly being American is no longer something you have to live down, something used to excuse the fact that you talk too loudly, dress too loudly, expect to have a cervical smear once a year, always ask if it's salad cream or mayonnaise, keep your bread and your beer in the fridge and get stroppy when the bus doesn't come, the post office won't let you have your lost post until you produce it as evidence, and someone tells you that if you wanted to see a really hot summer you should have been here in '76.

What's going on? My mother and I would like to know. Is this what they mean by one world?

'So what kind of Danish have you got?' my mother asked the waitress.

'Pineapple, raisin and chocolate,' said the waitress, a little worn down from the debate over the types of tea on offer.

'Chocolate?' repeated my mother, looking suspicious. 'A chocolate Danish?'

'That's right,' said the waitress grimly. 'Pineapple, raisin or chocolate.'

I smiled at the waitress. 'So what'll you have, Mom?'

'Cheesecake,' said my mother.

Typical. 'Mom,' I said, the soul of patience, 'Mom, I thought you said you had your heart set on a Danish. I thought you said you hadn't had a Danish in over three weeks and you were suffering from severe withdrawal symptoms.'

'I can't relate to chocolate Danish,' said my mother, sounding accusing and looking at me. 'We don't have chocolate Danish in America. We have cheese and we have prune, but we don't have chocolate.'

At the table next to us a thirtysomething man and his young daughter were sitting down. He was wearing Levis, a plaid flannel shirt, black Converse and designer stubble. She was wearing a denim skirt, an orange sweatshirt, serious multicoloured basketball boots and knee-high white socks.

'Mom,' I sort of moaned. 'Mom, this is not America.'

I watched the man and his daughter pick up their menus. My mother watched them pick up their menus. We heard the father say something about a nice cheese roll. We heard the girl mention chips.

'Thank God,' said my mother.

'Amen,' said I.

'So you do want the Danish or you don't want the Danish?' said the waitress.

Orlando Curioso

RUTH RICHARDSON

There are two Orlandos of which you may already know something. The first is a character in a favourite Virginia Woolf novel, who, though said to have been born in Elizabethan England, lived for several centuries and changed from man to woman somewhere along the way. The second appears in a sixteenth-century poem in which a distracted lover, Orlando, rushes around a forest, and thus gains the sobriquet *Furioso*. There are times when I think I might represent the result of an effort to clone human progeny from these two fictional characters. A lot of the time I feel as if I've lived for at least 200 years. Moreover, I seem to be burdened with a personality trait which leads me to traverse the forest of London's skyscrapers and back alleys distracted not with furiosity, but with *curiosity*.

Being as old as this notion suggests, it seems very fortunate that I'm able to earn a living in the curious occupation of historian. My energies are at present directed towards the creation of a catalogue and indexes to all the illustrations published in a Victorian architectural journal. There are thousands of them, mostly wood engravings. The amount of work involved is colossal – daunting, laborious, and enthralling all at once. To historians of architecture, and to

14

architects interested in the renovation of old buildings, the journal has long been a trusted friend; but among the general public it is very little known. I hadn't used it very much myself until a few years ago when I was appointed to the post I now hold. I had already met the Victorian journal's editor in another context, as the author of a series of books about life in Victorian slums which I'd used extensively in earlier researches. In fact it was only during work on the journal that it became clear to me that many chapters in his important slum books had appeared originally as investigative journalism.

The gentleman in question was appointed editor of the journal in 1844, only a few years after Victoria's accession to the throne, when he was in his early thirties. He remained in harness until he was past seventy years of age, having supervised publication of an issue every week of those forty years. The published results of his labours are imbued as much with his remarkable personality as with the architecture and opinions of his times. Much appreciated by his contemporaries, the journal's sales rose and rose during his editorship, and suffered a marked drop when he retired. It was read by all social classes, from Prince Albert downwards. Even building labourers read and acted upon his words – in 1871 the journal published a profound apology to several hundred of them who had arrived at the site of the new Law Courts in the Strand after the journal had announced, in good faith, the erroneous news that work was due to begin.

It's a strange experience knowing a person intimately for forty years who in fact died generations before one's own birth. Millions of his words have passed through my eye–brain nerve receptors. I've witnessed their author develop from a dashing young architect to an influential statesman

of architectural journalism. His voice is familiar from spee-
ches at public meetings and from evidence given before
Select Committees. His ideas have developed and matured
within my purview. His deep love of London has informed
and reinforced my own. I've seen him age and retire. And
there are things about his future afterlife of which he himself
was surely ignorant – his obituary notices, his beautiful
tomb in Brompton Cemetery, the blue commemorative
plaque on the outside of his old home, and his name carved
on the gold-medallists' wall at the Royal Institute of British
Architects. I cannot fathom, though, what he would have
thought of a curious young woman several generations his
junior, with short hair and breeches, so deeply involved in
his written words as to plant his grave with rosemary after
he had been lying boxed up and buried in it for a century
and more.

Over the last few years, as a result of his labours and my
own, I've been privileged to observe Victorian architecture
develop out of Georgian styles, the coming of the railways,
and the removal of Nash's colonnade all the way along the
Regent Street Quadrant. There was a market in architectural
antiques even then, and the sale of the columns has not been
missed. I've witnessed Queen Victoria's grand opening of
the Great Exhibition of All Nations at the Crystal Palace in
Hyde Park, and the removal of that great glass edifice to
Sydenham, where advanced water technology has been
designed to serve an impressive system of fire sprinklers, as
well as cascades and fountains. Gothic architecture has been
revived with great enthusiasm, and hundreds of churches,
free public libraries, museums and art galleries, schools,
baths and washhouses have been erected. New roads have
been cut through slum districts, and new sewers and underground railways dug. Industrial towns which only a gener-

ation ago weie little more than villages have been actively erecting fine civic buildings. New housing has crept its tentacles well into the green fields, but many green spaces – including Hampstead Heath – have been saved after stiff battles with landowners.

There's been a long-running debate about if and when a new architectural style shall emerge, and concurrently that exciting period of Victorian architectural eclecticism has flowered in which all previous styles are beautifully mixed up and set in stucco or baked in terracotta, to form a new style utterly unlike anything before or since. Interestingly the theorists who have spurned it haven't yet realised that this *is* the Victorian style. In the same period of time the gleaming Lloyd's building has appeared beside the shell of its previous home, postmodernism has developed, Richmond riverside and the Turner Gallery at the Tate have opened their doors, and Prince Charles has exhibited his Vision of Britain.

I've seen London itself change radically. The demolition of the Regent Street arcade is only one such change. I've sauntered with my Victorian journalist from Pedlar's Acre across old Westminster Bridge – well, it was old and crippled in 1851 – and have watched the moon's light illumine the towers of the Houses of Parliament, still under construction. I know what stone was used in the building, the identity of the contractors, and even how the great bell, now known as Big Ben, was hoisted up into the fine new Victoria Tower. Pedlar's Acre is the name which was given at that time to the site of what is presently known as County Hall, whose parapets in my lifetime have displayed huge banners quantifying London's unemployed in a flagrant and provocative taunt to those occupying the very building across the river still unfinished a sentence or two ago. In my Victorian editor's time, no central authority existed for London, although the need for such a thing was advocated forcefully in his pages on many an occasion. And, in my time, the great council for London which Victorians envisaged, formulated and eventually created with enormous pride in the year my editor friend died, has nurtured and educated millions of Londoners, including myself, and has disappeared.

My parents were always pointing things out to us as children, always sharing their love of London's history, so buildings, streets, monuments and the personality of districts have always been objects of curious interest. Growing up in any locality involves a store of memories often tied to particular places – so travelling through London, naturally enough, many such memories resonate. There are also echoes of haphazard snippets gleaned from books and from conversations with my parents and others of their generation about their childhood escapades, the Blitz, or the Festival of Britain.

One result of having worked so closely for so long on the Victorian journal, though, has been that the whole of the metropolis has taken on an unexpected and curious extra dimension for me. Not only do I see what I do in the normal way through my own corporeal eyes, here, now, or recall familiar memories of my own time past, I now also possess a bulging mental filing cabinet of knowledge from the pages of the journal's handsome old volumes. I meander round postmodern London like Virginia Woolf's Orlando, who carried into the twentieth century memories of seventeenth-century ice-fairs on the Thames. I feel rather like someone woken from one of those curious Victorian stereoscopic double pictures – the ones which need special glasses to bring their contents to life in all three dimensions. It's almost as if my NHS specs endowed X-ray vision to see through buildings, into the fourth.

London holds layers of strangeness for me now. Occasionally, the curious experience of overlayed time takes on a hallucinatory quality. Turning a corner I find I know exactly what should be there and isn't, or that I have a sudden recognition of a building I know inside and out from pictures and plans, but which I've never before set eyes upon in its actuality of brick, stone, carving and decorative ironwork.

Even familiar buildings take on a curious feel. I must have climbed the steps of the Albert Memorial a hundred times as a child, walking home from the museums with my sisters – taking the tour around it and looking at Albert sitting up there under his canopy. Folklore had it that one of the sculpted life-size figures in the bas-relief which circles the monument appeared twice, and that there was a secret trap door beside the duplicate by which one could press a button and get inside. Of course we never found the way in, even though we searched for it carefully on every visit.

I can't remember a time when I didn't love the Albert Memorial, partly because it was so familiar. Even in the everlasting snows of that terrible winter of 1962–3, when Sylvia Plath froze to death, it stood there like a darkly colourful Matterhorn amid the cold whiteness and greyness of the park. Everyone knew the Memorial commemorated a good person greatly loved, who suffered a needless early death. Through reading the Victorian journal, however, my affection for the building has deepened. I've developed an appreciation of the great intention behind the Memorial, which was – by bringing together the hands and brains of the finest metalworkers and sculptors and other craftworkers alive at the time – to create a monument for the era as much

19

as for the man it celebrated. One of the illustrations on which I've worked is a remarkable wood engraving of the cross which graces its loftiest pinnacle, engraved with such clarity that the wood engraver can be discerned reflected in the polished surface of its topmost jewel.

Our own era has cared for the monument so poorly that it's no longer possible for present-day children so much as even to know there's a frieze of figures round which to take a circuit. I suppose the folklore about the secret door has already died a death. Passers-by are informed that the Memorial, which is surrounded by a huge hoarding, is now a dangerous structure. But knowing the journey up the steps and around the frieze, and appreciating the energy and faith Victorians invested in it, I can sense the care in the chisel marks on every statue now unseen behind the hoarding – almost as if the furrows in the stone were in my own skin. Knowing precisely what the cross looks like close to, I feel as if I have flown over the barrier, up and over the canopy, and taken a very close look, like that dead wood engraver.

Despite its sorry state, the building still has an aura of Victorian pride and respect as it soars over the park. It all focuses on the cast statue of Albert, which, protected by its canopy, gazes out across the road to the enormous elliptical drum of the Royal Albert Hall of Arts and Sciences. Prior to reading the journal's coverage, I was oblivious to the fact that the fine terracotta frieze which runs round the famous hall was executed by women artists from the South Kensington School of Art. This knowledge imparts a glow of extra pleasure when contemplating the building from the bus stop across the road. Once again, sadly, our own era has been reckless of the care and thought invested by the Victorians in their buildings. Recent cleaning has affected the terracotta's surface in some way and the mortar is porous, so although

It's clean again it may now be vulnerable to damp and frost. Prayers are said in quiet churches that some expedient will emerge to rectify the situation.

There are times when I really ache to be able to discuss such things with my Victorian journalist. The development over several years of a deep respect for the views of someone who happens to be dead reinforces feelings of loss on such occasions, and of annoyance with Time for intervening so inconveniently. When you're in the habit of hearing someone's wise opinions on every past major architectural event, you miss them severely when something new happens. His views on the plans for the Mansion House block, the Broadgate site, the Isle of Dogs or the contending plans for Paternoster Square would, I know, be wise and intelligent – commentary entirely without the cliquey pretentiousness and self-serving of much modern architectural writing.

In a sense, though, I think I know what he would say. Reading his thoughtful editorials for forty years conveys an insight into how a new building or development might have been received. A great many of the buildings he wrote about still stand, and many's the time that I've been struck by the freshness of his observations upon them. Before the unveiling in 1874 of the new equestrian statue of Prince Albert at Holborn Circus, he offered the opinion that the statue might turn out to be rather small in scale for the situation in which it was intended to stand. I recently undertook an expedition specifically to see whether or not this view was justified, and was struck by its sagacity. The statue remains charming, but lost: nobody notices it.

Many of my Victorian editor's perceptions are over a century old, yet like that one, still hold true. In the case of Albert's statue they can be tested on living pulses, but a great number of the buildings discussed and illustrated in the journal no longer exist. Of course, some designs for buildings were published but never erected, save in the imagination. In other cases, buildings were not completed to plan. Should ever I become a millionaire, for example, I shall endow funds for the completion of All Saint's Church, Notting Hill, which exhibits in the journal the fine spire and flamboyant Victorian buttresses it never actually received. A slump in the building trade of the 1850s left the half-completed church standing forlornly for several years amidst roofless shells of houses in the fields of Notting Hill, causing it to be known locally as 'All Sinners in the Mud'. Several generations later, my grand-dad – a local carpenter and locksmith – fitted the blackout curtains to its ornamented windows during the Blitz. Thankfully, the spireless church survived, and a century after it was illustrated in the journal, it was still standing right beside my childhood home; its tolling bell woke me from sleep many a morning. Finding it illustrated in detail in the journal made me take binoculars along to see if the familiar windows were ever executed to the original design.

My grand-dad's careful efforts may have helped save 'All Sinners', but many of the other buildings illustrated, which were fully completed in bricks and mortar by Victorian hands, were later obliterated by bombs dropped from flying machines only dreamt of when they were a-building. Wartime newsreels showing London being blasted from the air fill me with a grateful amazement that anything survived. The same sort of process has been going on ever since upon the poor survivors, with the more insidious targeting of developers. Victorians of the same occupation called themselves 'improvers'. The intention seems to be more or less the same: to persuade all and sundry, by the use of a positive-sounding word, that *everything* done is a positive improvement. Yet sadly this hasn't been the case with our latter-day 'improvers'.

There's a passage in *Paradise Lost* in which Satan, disguised as the Serpent, endeavours to persuade Eve to try the apple. Part of his argument is to convince her of the miraculousness of the world and its fruits. In comparison with Heaven, he argues, Earth is actually much more wondrous and beautiful. Heaven was only God's first attempt at creation, and how could an all-powerful God create something less beautiful second time round? 'What God, after better, worse could build?' The fallen angel's argument is perfectly logical and very persuasive. And, though I have no present knowledge and little future prospect of experiencing heaven, I am prepared to believe that this planet really is the most beautiful place in the universe.

But what may be true for the Deity is clearly not so for humankind. It is certainly possible – we are surrounded daily with the evidence – for human beings to follow beauty with ugliness, and well-wrought buildings with rotten ones. One has only to compare the sturdy old buildings erected by the School Boards in the late nineteenth century with those plasterboard and asbestos-ridden structures with which some of them have unfortunately been replaced. While the first still have a noble appearance after having served many generations of teachers and children over the century since they were built, newer school buildings are already unfit for further use. The same is true of the model housing erected for the Victorian labouring classes and their high-rise twentieth-century equivalents. The old buildings were sturdily built and can withstand substantial alteration for a new lease of life; the new ones so flimsy as to be worthless for any type of conversion save demolition.

One of my Victorian editor's most deeply held convictions was that architecture reflects the state of the civilisation which produces it. Applied to our own century this important principle highlights the great deterioration of architectural standards which has occurred. If those sturdy schools and model houses reflect a desire to build fine buildings well, what do the rubbishy ones of our own era say about twentieth-century British civilisation? All too often post-war architecture is ugly, repetitive, insubstantial and above all, mean. Only in the last few years has any significant change become at all evident, and even now contradictory developments seem to be taking place. On the one hand there's a popular movement: a growing delight in the refurbishment of old buildings; and an appreciation of their scale and features has resulted in new buildings which echo architectural precedents the Victorians themselves would have recognised, understood and enjoyed. Fine buildings are appearing, like the Prince's Square development in Glasgow, which feature careful attention to detail, interesting human touches like hand-made ironwork and human-scale nooks and crannies. Counterpoising these changes, especially in city centres, are new, huge, ugly canyon blocks of offices, clad in dark brick or heavy-looking stone, which appear as if from nowhere, gobbling up ever more extensive areas of ground, and in their greedy appropriation obliterating old site boundaries and street patterns which took centuries to evolve.

For those who care about history, about the evolution of architecture, and about human scale in buildings and streets, the only defence against these monstrous edifices is the use of planning and listing legislation. But because so much financial capital and interest-yielding office space is involved in these 'developments' the way is fraught with difficulty. In many cases it fails altogether: witness the campaign in the spring and summer of 1989 to save the remains of the Rose Theatre. The timber and chalk ground-floor layer of the Rose had lain like a soft fossil in the mud of Bankside, almost undisturbed, beneath a series of buildings erected on the same site over the centuries since Shakespeare and Marlowe trod its boards. Then, between the demolition of one office block and the erection of a larger one – whose piles would certainly have obliterated most of whatever had survived the intervening centuries – a handful of archaeologists started to dig. Gradually the profile emerged of its stage, the pulverised hazel-shell surface of the pit where the audience stood, and the foundations of the galleries. All manner of objects also emerged, such as bear bones, Elizabethan shoes and coins – even a human skull – which had long lain quietly embedded in the mud, surviving even the Blitz.

At the time it was curious indeed to look at the antiquated old maps and panoramas of Southwark, to try to make out where the Elizabethan boundaries and alleys coincide with our present-day street plans. Maid Lane, which has been called the Shaftesbury Avenue of Elizabethan London because it gave access to all Southwark's open-air theatres, is now widened and known as Park Street. Over the last 150 years the riverside has been embanked, and a huge bridge has risen to span the Thames, its approach road wider than the little theatre beside which its traffic unknowingly passes. Many local alleys with colourful names like Love Lane, Hindes Alley and Mosses Alley have disappeared, but alongside the theatre Rose Alley narrowly remains – having borne that name since Shakespeare's day. When the theatre again became visible, it served as a touchstone for both eras, piercing through all pre-existing maps into our own time like a needle in a stack of punched cards, creating a verifiable point of consonance between old and new views.

The 'developers' were eventually induced to redesign their destructive piling, not by listing or the planning process, but by a mobilisation of public opinion, which coalesced protectively around the Rose with candle-lit vigils, lute music and readings from Elizabethan plays. We felt curiously akin to the peace campaigners of the 1960s, putting flowers down the barrels of guns. But we had about as much hope as had my grandfather when he put up the blackout curtains against the bombers. The archaeologists were ordered off the site before they could complete their work. Because of the lack of statutory protection, the theatre is now concreted over, piles have been driven through areas which might house its outer walls, and no one knows if it will ever again see the light of day. The most important building ever to have occupied that site could be lost for ever.

I suppose 'developers' have a variety of X-ray vision, too: a sort of Mammon-vision which endows no appreciation of present beauty or curiosity about past history, but is capable only of perceiving the possibility of a site's ever-increasing money-yield. Capacity is what counts, and new buildings with their repetitive, mean, inner dimensions and enormous exterior size offer a higher yield of cubic capacity. Sadly there remain architects and structural engineers who are happy to serve such masters. Old buildings, however beautiful, are merely an encumbrance to those with such incurious perceptions. The present dominion of this impoverished vision is doubly deleterious – its ridiculous rents surely contribute to economic inflation, and it strips our towns and cities of their history besides.

It seems to me to be a principle worth stating that even

when the demolition of an old building is agreed, no one should have the right to obliterate the fields beneath. The endeavour should always be to preserve old street patterns. In rare cases such as the Rose, developers should have to observe a stay of execution until the full archaeology is made known by careful excavation. Something as important as the Rose should rightfully be classified a national monument, and developers should be required to insure themselves against the discovery of such an 'encumbrance' on their site. No new building should be permitted if it might damage such a priceless find. If building there must be, then it should be constructed in such a way as to preserve such unique remains.

If the Victorians could do it, then why cannot we? One article in my Victorian journal concerns the discovery in the 1840s of a fine Roman floor during the construction of the Coal Exchange, which stood opposite Billingsgate in Lower Thames Street. Being the central place in London wherein all coal was bought and sold, the building was a very hub of commerce, but alongside its special wind-dial for calculating the arrival of coal shipments on the Thames' tides, the Roman find was appreciated as an asset rather than an encumbrance. The lower floor of this beautiful cast-iron and glass building – opened by Prince Albert – was redesigned around the discovery. The floor was again saved when the Victorian building was demolished in the 1960s, and it's now imprisoned in the basement of an office block on the same site.

The secret life of building sites is embedded in their boundaries and in their depth. *The fourth dimension is present in the other three.* A stone-age flint arrow-head, presently displayed in Glasgow City Museum, had been discovered in an urban garden. Of course not all gardens occupy the site of a stone-age hunt, and not every alley stands alongside a Shakespearian theatre, but all building sites have a history, and it's just this history that the new monster buildings are set to obliterate. Street patterns often follow the age-old boundaries of the fields beneath, which themselves often date back before Domesday to the natural contours of the ground, old streams or paths curving through long-felled woodlands.

In historical terms it doesn't seem all that long ago that a leading architectural journalist actually cared for the past as well as for the future: promoting in his weekly editorials the notion that we should build for the future as well as for the present; that we should save the past for the benefit of the future; and that the architecture of our own civilisation should be as beautiful in decay as are the ruins of ancient Greece or Rome.

During a discussion of what future archaeologists, trying to piece together our civilisation, might find from what we leave behind, my Victorian editor once observed that he

should be contented with the impression that would be given, if two or three houses [near Paddington] with the interior of which we happen to be tolerably well acquainted, were sealed up with lava from a neighbouring Vesuvius for the examination of the antiquaries from New Zealand or elsewhere, who may be seeking in a distant age to know something of the homes and inner life of the English in the nineteenth century.

It was only after reading and enjoying these words that I first visited Linley Sambourne House. A fine middle-class Victorian home, sealed as if with lava from a Vesuvius in the neighbourhood of Kensington High Street, the house is open to the public under the kindly auspices of the Victorian Society. Saved by a family who could not bring themselves to change the building and its contents from its original 1870s décor and furnishings, it comes as close to my editor's desideratum as anyone could desire.

Like the rain forests, nothing will survive unless we think again about what it means to be custodians of the past for the future. We still have a wealth of history to pass forward to future generations, and a duty to save what we can from needless destruction. It is deeply pleasing to hear, as I did the other day, that a new housing scheme at Spitalfields is about to restore the old street patterns after the demolition of a crumbling modern block.

But I wouldn't have *all* ugly blocks demolished and replaced with beautiful buildings on old street patterns. At least one should be saved. Perhaps a fair impression could be given of the officially sanctioned destruction of neighbourhoods since the last war only by saving a larger area than a single building. In order to offer the full context for such an exemplary edifice I therefore propose that the town centre of Hoddesdon in Hertfordshire be declared a national monument. Until 1965 Hoddesdon was an ordinary little country town with a thriving market-place and a delightful bustling atmosphere. For some unknown reason it attracted the visionaries of cubic capacity, who arranged for its heart to be removed and for concrete to be laid metres thick over the wound. Through-traffic has since been siphoned off by a bypass, and the now deserted concrete centre has been colonised by dripping stalactites and lichens, blowing litter, and those who cannot flee anywhere else. Even if the sealing with local lava of the entire town centre was to be avoided, evacuation to another locality would be a mercy for the townsfolk.

The monument should, if it will, stand for all time as a sort of exemplary national edifice for the benefit of present and future architects, planners, council employees, politicians, economists, geographers, historians and archaeologists. Indeed, I would go so far as to suggest that all children studying the new national curriculum for history should be actively encouraged to visit Hoddesdon. The visit could serve many useful educational functions. Children could learn by rote the facts of the case for later testing: most buildings of note in the vicinity demolished; a nine-storey grey concrete block on stilts erected by E.S. Boyer & Partners 1965–6. An appreciation of the long evolutionary process of British architecture could be imparted. Organic forms of urban development could be examined, and the effect upon them of the mid-twentieth century onslaught of old Mammon-eyes could be charted.

Interdisciplinary topics thrown up by the visit could usefully be raised, such as the similarities and differences between a British market-place and a British shopping centre, and the varieties of enterprise each hosts. Some pupils might enjoy a consideration of the mid-twentieth century eclipse of older architectural materials, forms, skills and detailing. Scientific students could examine the chemical properties of stalactites, concrete cancer, or the biological colonisation of damp concrete by lichens and mosses. The artistically-inclined could be invited to explore the visual contrasts in colour, shape and form between green fields, trees, old buildings and repetitive grey concrete features. Imaginative pupils could be allowed to experience Orlando Curiosoism – to stray, as it were, into the fourth dimension.

Perhaps the local library will make available artefacts unearthed during the 1960s pile-driving, and maps whereby the original street and field shapes can be discerned under the concrete. Copies of contemporary local and national newspapers could be made available as an aid to teachers, and important tendencies of that era – such as Rachmanism and Poulsonism – could be raised for debate. Perhaps, since the passage of almost thirty years will soon be up, real 1960s documentation – contemporary council records – could be made accessible for analysis by older children, by which those who commissioned the monument can be identified, and their motives examined and discussed.

Curious young students will surely learn a great deal about the nature of history from the investigation.

Bloody Foreigners

ANNE CENDRE

All my life I have been a foreigner. I have never been a resident in a country of which I hold a passport by right of birth or marriage. That makes me a born outsider and observer. It seems natural therefore that I chose journalism as a profession.

This also confirms my view that it is possible to have roots in countries other than one's own. My deepest roots are in Geneva, the city where I was born and where I spent my first quarter of a century. Since I appeared to be completely at home there, I was never asked if I was Swiss and it did not seem to matter. I could not vote, but neither could Swiss women, who only got the right to vote on federal matters in 1971.

When I decided to broaden my horizon which was seemingly blocked by the Swiss Alps, I went to work in New York. After only a few months there, and in spite of my accent and rudimentary knowledge of the language, I was repeatedly asked not whether but when I was going to apply for United States' citizenship. My negative reply gave rise to astonishment. The Americans did not understand that joining their great land was not necessarily my life's ambition.

32

Now in the United Kingdom, things are a bit different again. Although I have lived here for about twenty years, nobody has ever suggested that I should try to become a subject of Her Gracious Majesty. It is not because I am either coloured, or black, or otherwise handicapped, it is simply because the British never would say such a thing. They do not intrude in private matters of any kind.

Just as well, since I have no intention of embarrassing the Home Office by adding my name to their endless list of people seeking British citizenship. In saying so I do not want to offend anybody, certainly not the wretched officials who have the unenviable task of separating the wheat from the chaff according to the convoluted laws of British nationality.

Even if they do not say so to your face the British are incredibly proud of their country. 'There can be no doubt that we live in the most beautiful, most tolerant and most politically mature of countries.'[1] 'We have the best burglars in Europe.'[2] 'Britain's air transport industry is the envy of the world.'[3] 'Britain, the most sophisticated democracy in the world.'[4] Britain has 'the best professional army in the world.'[5]

Surely many nations think they are the best. But the British are the only people who regard themselves with such awe that they give a capital letter to the first person singular, as they do when they refer to the Head of State, the members of the Church and the aristocracy. I, the King, the Archbishop and the Duke are equally respectable. The Germans give a capital letter to 'you' (*Sie*) and 'yours' (*Ihr*). So do the Dutch and the Italians.

When the British refer to foreigners they do so with some contempt. National qualifications have often a derogatory connotation. It is rude to take 'French leave.' But the French retaliate in finding it very impolite to *filer à l'anglaise.*

(Fortunately there are some redeeming expressions, mostly erotic: the French letter, the French kiss and French polish.) Spanish practices infuriate London press barons. The Dutch are considered mean since they invite you to 'go Dutch' or have a 'Dutch treat'. Anyone who talks gibberish talks 'double Dutch'. And if one sees only small portions of blue in the sky, they are 'Dutch breeches'. There must, however, be a good word for the 'Dutch cap'.

Unflattering nicknames are sometimes given to foreigners: the frogs, the krauts, the wogs, the wops, the gooks sound rather unpleasant; terms such as wallabies, paddies, nips may sound a little kinder, but are equally unpleasant. Insults are occasionally hurled at people whose physical appearance is different. My husband who is French, and certainly does not look English, was once abused in venomous tone by a total stranger who was definitely English: 'You Arab cunt!'

On the other hand, the British people can be extremely nice and helpful when a foreigner asks questions in the street, even when they seem to have great difficulty understanding the accent. They always look surprised that it is possible not to know English as well as they do.

The British have no incentive to learn foreign languages. Why should they? The whole world wants to speak English. However, some newspapers insist on using Herr, M (when it should actually be M.), and Senor, Senhor or Signor, and their female counterparts, when they could write plainly Mr or Mrs. This strange custom only applies to the five great European languages. When the British occasionally try other tongues it can lead to hilarious results and foreign quotations are almost always misspelled. (But that happens in most newspapers around the world.)

Foreign languages also appear regularly on restaurant

menus (again with frequently funny results). Since the British admit that their cooking is no good they try to hide the fact by using French terms to describe quite ordinary, boring, unimaginative dishes. Unfortunately their *cuisine* is no better than their cooking, even though their food may be superb.

Fashion is another area in which the British feel slightly inferior, so fashion shows abroad receive a fairly large coverage in the British press, and *haute couture* foreigners such as Christian Dior, Saint Laurent, Cardin, Hermès, Valentino, Ferragamo, Emmanuel Ungaro, or Issey Miyake have established bridge-heads in Bond Street and Sloane Street.

It would be possible to encourage people's sense of discovery if there were more translations of books and plays available. Besides Chekhov and Ibsen non-British theatre is rarely performed. Who but the most dedicated theatre-goer has seen the best contemporary, let alone classical, French, Spanish, Italian or German masterpieces? Anouilh used to be very popular, but who has heard of Montherlant or Marcel Aymé? Lorca is fairly well known but what about Alberti? Pirandello is given a rare airing, Diego Fabbri never. Peter Weiss was discovered by Peter Brook through the famous *Marat-Sade* play, since then nothing; Brecht, the greatest of the twentieth-century dramatists, is still considered élitist. I would like to quote more recent authors but I have lived in Britain so long that I am completely out of touch with developments on the Continent.

Outside London, not many foreign-language films are screened in Britain. Even here the choice is pretty limited compared to other European capitals. The latest international film-makers are only available to the happy few at the National Film Theatre, whereas American films flood the British market. Who knows the best films of Italy,

Germany, France, Spain, South America, let alone Japan or Eastern Europe? In the video shops foreign titles are non-existent. The public does not want to make the effort of reading subtitles, and since it is assumed that foreign films attract few people the distribution companies do not go to the expense of dubbing them. Only the Brigitte Bardot vehicles were popular enough to be post-synchronised in English.

Listening all day to British and American music on radio and records, youngsters on the Continent learn some English without effort. Young people here are never exposed to pop in other languages. While they have the opportunity to learn in numerous evening classes, the British do not frequent them as assiduously as foreigners. I have certainly noticed in the foreign language classes I have attended that the number of British students was smaller and their tendency to drop out greater.

When the European Community decided to organise a programme for improving the teaching of foreign languages, the Thatcher government refused to participate. The British will have the Conservatives to thank for indulging their linguistic laziness. Anyway it has never been a 'done thing' here to show one's intellectual abilities. 'The English are constitutionally anti-intellectual.'[6]

It must be reassuring to be able to accuse others for one's own failures. If it can be shown for instance that the unacceptable face of capitalism is all the fault of foreigners who do not understand the game and who are not gentlemen, so much the better. Is Tiny Rowland not a German called Roland Fuhrhop? Is Ernest Saunders not an Austrian called Ernst W. Schlayer? Is Mohamed Al-Fayed not an Egyptian called Mohamed Fayed?

On the other hand, when they succeed, foreigners are

accepted, albeit with condescension. The flamboyant and slightly mad Robert Maxwell is of course a Czechoslovak called Ian Hoch. By the way, speaking of newspapers, is it not surprising that many of the big proprietors are of foreign origin? The Astors were American, Beaverbrook, Thomson and Black are Canadian, Murdoch is Australian–American. They are activated by the idea that with such a weapon they can penetrate the British Establishment and create a power base. Apart from Beaverbrook, who became Minister of Information during the Second World War, the others do not yet appear to have realised their political ambitions.

On the strength of these examples, it can be stated that the British actually welcome foreigners. (I will not mention racism because I believe that there is not more racism here than in most other European countries.) But it should be stressed that all the examples I have given come from the white Commonwealth. So do quite a number of prominent businessmen and politicians. The links with the Commonwealth are still very strong, as with one's own family. They seem more natural than with Europe, which has long been the traditional adversary. But I suspect the main reason for sympathy towards the Commonwealth is the usage of a common language. If Salman Rushdie had not been an Indian who had studied in Britain would he have received the life-saving help he now enjoys?

Leaving aside high political or industrial circles, the British attitude towards foreigners is slightly different. As a member of the foreign press I have always been well received when I ask for information. People are polite and helpful whenever possible. But they are not really interested. It does not matter a jot to them what is written about Britain abroad. Nor does it interest them to know about us or our countries. Their ignorance of foreign history and geography is amazing. They don't think that it might be of any relevance to them. 'We cannot bring ourselves to believe it possible that a foreigner should in any respect be wiser than ourselves.'[7]

Of course, Switzerland is a small country, but it has many claims to fame, besides its bankers and Zurich gnomes. Nevertheless Switzerland is generally confused with Sweden. Now I happen to think that it would be worthwhile for the British to know something about the Swiss political system, which is accepted by its people and seems after all to work pretty well.

The Swiss constitution, with its decentralised powers, referendums and proportional representation, could be an example for others. It could solve some of the problems in Ireland and Scotland. However, its consensus politics is never understood in Britain, where confrontation seems to be the accepted norm. When I tell British politicians that conservatives, socialists and even communists sit comfortably side by side in local governments in Geneva and other Swiss towns, they can hardly believe it.

The fact that Great Britain is an island must be the explanation. Since they have lost their empire the British have retreated into their own territory and many would prefer to close the door to the rest of the world.

The British sometimes have to admit, however, that foreign lands can have advantages – the sun, for one thing – so they do go abroad. And what do they prefer? Islands. Amongst favourite places for their holidays or retirement are the Balearic and the Canary Islands, Corfu, Malta, and the Bahamas. But they try to avoid mingling with local people. Moreover they do not like the local customs or foods and demand hamburgers and chips.

'Abroad is unutterably bloody and foreigners are fiends.'[8]

38

The exploits of hooligans in Majorca or the Costas (or even
in British coastal towns) stems from their disdain for people
they do not care to know or understand. Why do they react
in such a violent way? Clearly it is not only because they
drink too much and tend to move in packs like wolves.
Young people need to give vent to their energy, their
vitality, and if they have no safety valve they will behave
aggressively even when events do not warrant it. In Switzerland – if I may return to the experience of this tiny country
which has proved its durability, since it will celebrate next
year the 700th anniversary of its foundation – an outlet does
exist. It is called military service.

There are of course several classes of foreigners in Britain.
Being a European Community national, I happen to be in
a privileged category. I am able to live, buy a flat, and work
here without a special permit. I also pay my taxes here,
which is indeed a privilege since they are higher in Switzerland from where I get my income.

The rebates are good, the expense allowances fairly generous. Unemployment benefits and pensions are lower than
elsewhere in the European Community but that does not as
yet affect me personally. What I object to is the poll tax,
unfair to most people, not least to foreigners.

The poll tax is supposed to enable the electorate to control
the activities of local councils: electors can sack councillors
if they think they pay too much for the services they receive.
Well, as a foreigner I cannot vote, so I cannot endorse or
protest against council spending and I still have to pay the
poll tax. In Holland and Denmark residents who are EC
nationals may vote in local elections. Perhaps this will
eventually be adopted here. A House of Lords' select committee has recommended that EC nationals of more than

two years' residence may be allowed to vote in Britain. I might see that in my lifetime.

Will I also ever see the Channel Tunnel? The manner in which the British talk about it almost gives reason to doubt that it will finally be built although the digging continues hopefully. It would seem that most British people would prefer it to be sunk without trace.

As a foreigner, it is difficult to believe that this possible first ever fixed link with a foreign country, this extraordinary feat of engineering, this easy and rapid access to the Continent which will eliminate the hazards of meteorology elicits such hatred amongst the British. Can it be fear? Fear of a military invasion? But surely blocking a tunnel is simpler than protecting borders and closing a frontier.

No, the main objection must be that the British are terrified of being swamped by 'bloody foreigners'.

To conclude, I hope it has been noticed that not once have I used the word 'xenophobia'.

NOTES

[1] John Mortimer, *Sunday Times*, 13 November 1983.
[2] *Daily Telegraph*, 29 November 1983.
[3] Nicholas Ridley in the House of Commons, 5 June 1985.
[4] Gerald Kaufman, BBC, 14 February 1987.
[5] Roy Hattersley, BBC, 29 May 1987.
[6] Jonathan Miller, *The Times*, 21 March 1990.
[7] Anthony Trollope, *Orley Farm*, Oxford, Oxford University Press, 1985.
[8] Nancy Mitford, *The Pursuit of Love*, Harmondsworth, Penguin, 1970.

Homeownership – The Sale of the Century

EVA FIGES

During the eighties owning property became a British obsession, and at the close of the decade it reached mania proportions, with the inevitable aftermath – high interest rates, a housing slump, and repossessions. The decade began with the Government shutting down much of our productive industry, and people with money to invest began to put it, not into business, but into bricks and mortar. At middle-class parties the talk was all of rising house prices, with people boasting *ad nauseam* about the increasing value of their real estate. Any hint of change which might depress house prices was considered bad news by those with the good fortune to own a roof over their heads, regardless of the plight of those without one. House prices became far more important than earnings, as those with property grew richer and those without could find no way to get on the first rung of the 'housing ladder'.

A roof over one's head is surely a basic necessity of life. If any other essential commodity were suddenly subject to 30% inflation nobody would be crowing about it. Governments would fall, there might be rioting. But housing does not count in the general equation, because it is considered an investment, not a necessity. Rent rises are taken into account, as are mortgage interest rates, although a beleaguered government, having encouraged the population to buy rather than rent, would prefer interest rates not to count.

Deep in the Tory mentality is the idea that if the poor are disadvantaged it is all through their own fault. They are feckless, they do not make the right decisions. So, encourage them to buy their own homes and own shares and they can soon be as prosperous as the upper classes, instead of being a drain on the taxpayer. The fact that the middle classes do not often get made redundant overnight, to stay unemployed for years, the fact that most of them have good educations and a bit of capital in the bank is conveniently forgotten. Unfortunately, lured by Tory promises of a better life, many of the underprivileged have also forgotten these basic facts. And even those with reasonable prospects of a decent life, the educated young, have been duped into forgetting that in a capitalist free-for-all, capital is king. Many people simply do not understand just how rich the rich really are, just as the well-to-do do not begin to fathom what it is to be really poor.

The Thatcher Government got round the problem of people not having the wherewithal to join the prosperous middle classes by giving things away. They forced local councils to sell their housing stock at huge discounts. They privatised nationalised industries and public services in such a way that an overnight profit was assured. For the nation it was a catastrophe but for the people with the ability and the will to cash in on the situation it meant a sudden windfall.

Of course none of this has anything to do with real investment, whether in shares or housing. The people who bought shares sold, for the most part, on the first day of trading. (Many of them had to anyhow, having bought with borrowed money!) Council tenants who were virtually given their council houses bought, not for the security that homeownership is supposed to give, but to sell at a profit as soon as they legally could. At a time of depressed wages and high unemployment all this led to a false sense of prosperity, as people spent their winnings in this bingo economy. Consumerism boomed, retail outlets and service industries flourished for a while, giving a false sense of a 'transformed economy'.

Banks and building societies also seemed to be gripped by this general sense of euphoria. In my youth getting a second mortgage meant you were really on the slippery slope. Now people were encouraged to 'release the equity in your home', which meant borrowing money on the purely notional value of your home (since a house is only worth what someone is prepared to pay for it at any given time) and spending the loan on virtually anything you fancied – a second home, a second holiday, a second car.

And so a nation which had largely ceased to meet its own consumer needs, let alone export abroad, went on a spending binge that has resulted in the biggest trade deficit in our history. And all this from the grocer's daughter who believes in good housekeeping. Not only is the nation in debt, but private individuals now have more debt per head than ever before.

This is a government that is only able to think in the short term, about quick returns, which is why they have totally neglected long-term investment, such as transport, education, research and development. They have encouraged their electors to do the same, buying to sell and thus bringing about a huge increase in stockbrokers and estate agents.

Somehow in the last ten years people have forgotten that what really counts is working for a living. In the long term market forces must apply to housing as to everything else, and if house prices bear no relation to wages and salaries they must be brought into line. Add to this that in the last few years so many people bought property, not to live in, but as an investment, and some kind of slump seems inevitable.

This would not be so terrible if people actually owned their houses, but many do not. The Government has encouraged people to buy, almost regardless of their personal circumstances, and to do so with borrowed money. Couples who hardly knew each other rushed into joint ownership for the sake of double tax relief. People with insecure job prospects took out vast mortgages, and so on.

Part of the illusion is in the word itself: homeownership. Mrs Thatcher keeps trotting it out with great pride. But of course, if you buy a house with a 100% mortgage you do not own the house at all. What you have is a massive debt, subject to variable interest rates over most of your working life, and if you default for two months your creditors can repossess. Note the word. It is their house, they hold the deeds, and they are fully entitled to move in if you cannot meet your obligations. It is sad that so many people have falsely equated this kind of 'homeownership' with security. How many people have traded in a lifelong, guaranteed council tenancy for this kind of security, and now face repossession orders? Why, some of the poor mutts, dazzled by Tory propaganda, had not even budgeted for roof repairs, let alone interest rate rises! Let alone redundancy, a sick wife who has to give up work, or any of the other ills that man is heir to. And so a dream of double glazing and carriage lamps at the door turns into a nightmare of homelessness – two minutes in court is all it takes.

The ideal of owning one's own home has always been a bit of a British obsession. Well-to-do foreigners who rent all their lives and think nothing of it, do not understand our way of thinking. It was not always so in this country. The Victorians so often referred to by our rulers mostly rented, the rich in Knightsbridge and Park Lane, the poor elsewhere. Even Mr Pooter had a landlord, though today's Pooters would not be seen dead in rented accommodation. Why, only the other day I heard a young woman refer proudly to the fact that she was buying her two rooms in Brixton whilst a well-known journalist only rented his apartment in Eaton Square. The fact that she was having to pay half her income for this dubious privilege did not seem to come into the equation. But this is how the British view the matter.

To this day developed countries with a higher standard of living than our own have a much lower rate of owner occupation than Britain. Surely this should tell us some-thing? In 1979, when the Tories came into power, 57% of British homes were owner-occupied, and now it is 68% and rising. In West Germany the figure is 40%, in France 52%, in Italy it is 59% and in the USA it is 63% and falling. Since the only countries with which the UK stands comparison are Ireland (74%), Spain (77%), Greece (72%) and Bangladesh (90%) one is forced to the obvious conclusion that there is an inverse relationship between homeownership and stan-dards of living.

And it is not hard to see the reason why. These countries with high levels of homeownership still have large peasant communities, where houses are passed down from gener-ation to generation. These peasants may fear crop failure or flooding, but they do not have to worry about mortgage arrears in a bad year. An industrial society requires mobility of labour, and homeownership does not encourage people to move to new labour markets. Instead homeowners demand pay rises when interest rates go up, and who can blame them? Tory ministers may tell the unemployed to get on their bikes to find work, but new homeowners cannot do that. The difference in property values makes it impossible to sell a house in an area of high unemployment and start afresh where the work is. Even professional people are finding it impossible to move. When my son's old school appointed a new headmaster a few years ago he changed his mind about taking up the post because of property prices in London, although he was already living in the south-east. Is it any wonder the teacher shortage has reached crisis proportions? Or that local authorities have many vacancies they cannot fill? Or that the London Underground is so short of drivers that the service is becoming skeletal? Where are these people, whose earnings have been kept down for a decade as a matter of policy, supposed to live once council housing has been sold off and there is nothing else they can afford? You may think yourself fortunate to own a house that is worth half a million, even though you would have to die in order to collect, but this is of little use to you if the essential services on which we must all rely start to break down. Lack of investment in public transport meant that middle-class homeowners took to their cars. Now there are hopeless traffic jams and road schemes threaten the very existence, let alone the value of the property that those in work were so eager to get themselves in hock for. Hell has no fury like a property-owning democracy on the war-path, as every Tory backbencher knows. 'Not in my backyard' is the other side of the coin of a philosophy which holds that 'everything goes'.

If Thatcherism has now run out of steam it is because those people who did not object to her philosophy on moral grounds are now finding it will not work on practical grounds. No man is an island, or, put it another way, we all live on the same island and it is extremely small. The mess in somebody else's backyard will eventually spill over into mine. We have to invest in people, not just bricks and mortar, because eventually our lives and their quality depends on them, on their skills and good will. We also depend on their purchasing power. A house is only worth what someone else will pay for it. And too many rats in the sewers are not a good idea either – nothing puts such a damper on house prices as an outbreak of plague.

Meanwhile, what has this Tory dream of homeownership left us with? An uncontrolled consumer and credit explosion as people felt rich, not because their wages had gone up, but because the notional value of their homes had risen. Tenants have been put on the defensive as never before by landlords anxious to capitalise on the situation. One murderous, Rachman-type landlord publicly referred to his tenants as 'scumbags' and the police could not get a jury to convict him for his mafia exploits. The idea that mere tenants stand in the way of bingo prizes as yet undreamed of by human avarice has entered the British consciousness, so that being a mere tenant is as bad as being a welfare 'scrounger', even though you may have been paying too much for too little for thirty years whilst your leaky roof changed hands time and again. (Of course no Tory voter thinks that private tenants should have the right to buy – that would be contrary to the principle of private property, instead of merely defrauding the taxpayer.) We also have ghost villages created by the rich getting richer and buying second homes. There's no attempt, of course, to stop this individualist bandwagon through property taxes, either by penalising second homes or by taxing the profits on a house resold within a certain time. Instead the rates are replaced by the poll tax, which makes it cheaper than ever before to accumulate property. I understand the Prince of Wales will be saving over £10,000 a year in rates. Cottage owners will also do quite nicely, whilst young locals are unable to afford anything in the area where they and their parents grew up.

As usual there are more losers than winners in this cruel bingo game which gambles, not for plastic toys, but the very fabric of people's lives. Apart from food, shelter is the most basic necessity, and cannot be left to market forces. Every civilised country in the world recognises that, but we have lost even the veneer of civilisation. Thousands of people sleep on our streets every night; hundreds of thousands are forced into the misery of bed and breakfast accommodation, which costs the taxpayer far more than council housing. And who gets all this money? Private enterprise, of course, people providing slum accommodation which no environmental health officer would normally pass if he had any choice in the matter. But he no longer has. No new council housing, and the old stock sold off to catch votes and break up Labour strongholds. And those buyers who cannot keep up the mortgage payments and have their old council house repossessed may be deemed to have made themselves 'wilfully homeless', and get no help from a desperate authority. There is a rough justice in that, but it is rough.

Now slump has followed the uncontrolled boom. New luxury development stands empty, finding no buyers. Some of it is now occupied by the homeless, and there is a rough justice in that too. I hope they enjoy their jacuzzis. I wish them joy of their yuppie neighbours, suddenly back amongst the ordinary people they strove so hard to get away from, and complaining mightily about the fall in their investment. But then empty houses all around don't do much for your investments either. No man is an island, and from 1992 Britain will not be an island either – homeowners would do well to remember that. Houses are subject to the laws of supply and demand like everything else, and I suspect that after 1992 many of our skilled professionals, given new choices, will choose to work in Europe, and turn their backs on rat-infested, litter-strewn streets clogged with traffic, where public transport is expensive and scarcely functioning, where life-saving emergency services have almost ceased to exist, and where property is grossly over-priced compared to the rest of Europe. Add this to the demographic time-bomb of fewer school leavers in the 1990s, i.e., fewer first-time buyers, and the present slump could turn into an avalanche. There is always Hong Kong, of course, to save the homebuyer's bacon, but the party that believes in private property as a sacred cow also believes in Britain for the British, so a lot of potential buyers will have to look elsewhere.

Meanwhile, a lot of young people who cannot remember a time when Mrs Thatcher was not in power, have become homeowners. They will be paying too much for too little for many years to come. I hope they learn something from this expensive lesson, not just about the nature of capital, but about the need to control it. Individualism has its place, but at a basic level the human race depends on social values as surely as the proverbial honey-bee. The 1980s were an expensive aberration in our history, for which most of us have paid dearly, and will continue to pay dearly for many years to come. It needed a world war to establish the welfare state, and perhaps a generation with no direct memory of the conditions that brought it into being needed to have the clock turned back to find out what life can be like without it. It has been an expensive lesson, and the people who are really paying the price are not doing so in high mortgages, but in far more damaging ways. Put Adam Smith back in the ground where he belongs and let us try to get back from the eighteenth century to the last decade of the twentieth. The twenty-first is almost upon us. The building society may be generous with second mortgages, but history is not usually so generous with second chances.

Kilburn High Road

MELISSA BENN

Kilburn, the early months of 1990; the months of the gales, the ambulance strike, Mandela's release, the poll-tax riots.

Most Saturday mornings in Kilburn Square an evangelical preacher stands on the benches outside W.H. Smith and lectures to passers-by. A tall slim man, handsome, with a full black beard touched with white, he could be anywhere between 35 and 50. Wearing a white plastic life-jacket with 'GOD IS ALIVE' stencilled front and back he holds a Bible in his hand as he shouts. Most people skirt around him, blank-faced. Teenagers sneer out loud, 'You're fecking mad, mate.' Those who stop to listen do so warily, keeping a good twenty-feet distance. The preacher's manner is haranguing; he *is* probably mad. Yet I watch him debate with a woman – in private as it were, down on ground level – and I am struck by his courtesy and his engagement. Like the best of politicians he is utterly without cynicism about the tedious work of persuasion and conversion. The very eagerness of his expression betrays the fact that he is giving of something more important than himself. He is giving of his ideas and his time, because he believes it will contribute to the greater good.

So it is with the sellers of left-wing papers who stand

dotted around the symbolic centre of the Square, side by side with the commercial – the market that sells cheap jeans, jackets and jewellery, the fruit and vegetable stall, the young man with a clutch of Mickey Mouse and Donald Duck helium balloons in his left hand, a book in his right. Above all their heads the black painted slogans: VICTORY TO THE IRA. DEATH TO BRITISH IMPERIALISM. FREE THE BIRMINGHAM SIX. LONG LIVE MAOISM. RIM SPTRS.

The *Morning Star* Communists, the Peruvian Maoists, the Socialist Workers Party, the Revolutionary Communist Party. They stand and call, as dogged but less bold than the market-stall holders. Their problem is that people are long used to Thatcherism as an abstract outrage. The rehearsed anger of Socialist Worker headlines leave them unmoved. Not so the cause that can speak in specific images, the images of brother, sister, daughter and son. Like the miners and the nurses before them, the ambulance workers have staked out a very particular place for themselves in the public conscience. They are there, in the Square, all the winter with cold noses and rattling buckets, their anoraked bodies plastered with 999 labels, and, 'I SUPPORT MY AMBU-LANCE SERVICE.' And because everyone knows their story as if it were their own, they stop and talk and drop money. The ambulance workers are always surrounded, wreathed in smiles.

*

Kilburn High Road must be nearly a mile long. It is nearly always a dull grey – even in high summer – scrappy with litter, shit, squashed cans and crisp packets. Except for the red and purple blaze of late sunset when it is beautiful as only cityscapes can be.

Each part of what bounds Kilburn describes some section

within it: the suburban frontages of Edgware and Finchley begin their long runs up the back of the High Road, Willesden way; the high rises characteristic of the poorer estates of Notting Hill are dotted down the Brent side of the High Road; the money and middle-class tastes of Hampstead and St John's Wood are present in scattered but solid sections of gentrified terraces all around it. And yet, to approach Kilburn from this north-west end is to make a particular transition now common to all big cities; in this case from the rich respectable of one class to the poor respectable of another; from white to migrant; from empty to crowded. The wide streets of St John's Wood are another world, a world of single car doors slamming and an eerily calm silence. What you notice first and last is the solidity of the buildings and the spaces between them. There is no evidence of multi-occupation, the carved-up insides of an outer shell, signified by the stack of name cards to the right of the house bell. Single families still live in whole houses here and on the street, the pink-and-white of may blossom, early this year, blends with and complements the pink-and-white cake fronts of these intact residences.

To come down the hill to Kilburn from Hampstead is to be struck by another difference, a difference in skin tone. It is to notice how well and *shining* and strong the people in the latter look, walking with the kind of ease that can come only from the possession of resources for self-maintenance, that complicated equation of time and money which applies to bodies as well as to buildings. It's not that they move any faster in Hampstead High Street than they do in Kilburn High Road but that they move with a reserve power; the conscious knowledge of resources at the back of them; class.

*

I came to Kilburn ten years ago in March. For the first three years I lived in a rented basement flat, two rooms, bleak and coldly dark in the back. The address; 7a Victoria Road; it was just off the High Road, two minutes walk from the Square. One of my elder brothers had lived in the flat before me, my younger brother lived there after. In my head I can still hear my elder brother saying '7a': the fondly proprietorial shorthand we all used to signify pride at the continuity we had managed as a family, even into our twenties. A little to the left of the flat's front window was the cavernous entrance to an NCP underground car park, next to that a public toilet where shadowy figures hung out day and night. Up on the corner, the Grange Furniture Store, converted in the early eighties to make way for the ubiquitous red and yellow of McDonalds, faces the Abbey National Building Society.

I have a photo of myself taken that long ago, my back against the mirrored glass of the Abbey National, my friend David squinting behind his fringe and his camera, and beyond, the Grange Furniture Store, a shop whose very name evokes images of a different commercial past. The Grange was proof of a time when Kilburn was more moneyed than it has become; linking, if only symbolically, the West End to the north. And offering furniture I associate with grandmothers and their friends, the houses of people born in the Victorian era; brown, solid and dull.

That photograph is a favourite now, precisely because of the strangeness of each element within it. I know David no more, nor this Grange Furniture Store vision of the Kilburn High Road, nor that self in a crumpled red shirt, blown about hair and vainly pouting mouth who arches her back against the glass of the building society.

*

Migration is the key to the all-change of all cities, post-war.

54

With Camden, Kilburn was a centre for post-war Irish immigration. The men came to work in the munitions factories, the construction industry, coal mining, metal manufacture and agriculture. The women came to work as nurses in the hospitals or in domestic service. Mrs D down my road earned her living by cleaning houses for the rich who lived in the bigger houses in Kilburn. Jobs were easy to get but the pay was shocking. Father Warren, a priest at the Roman Catholic Church of the Sacred Heart, himself a recent migrant from Dublin, tells me how many young Irish men still come looking for work – mostly in the building trade. 'No matter how many times they are told in Dublin or any other town not to come without the equivalent of a thousand pounds, they still arrive, often empty-handed.' The church runs one hostel for young men, or it can direct arrivals to high-priced, private, rented accommodation. Rooms in Kilburn can cost anything from £50–£70 weekly, often sharing with two or three others. Luckier ones might have relatives or friends with floors to sleep on. It's not so lonely that way.

My neighbour, Marie Sargent is a small woman with neatly done auburn hair and eyes that see. Whenever I visit her, she always gives me special tea and toasted tea cakes and answers all my questions. This time, too. She arrived in 1960 when her eldest son, having finished college, was offered a job in engineering. A widow, she brought the other two – a son and daughter – to live here with her. She got a job almost immediately in the accounts section of a large department store on the High Road, B.B. Evans, now demolished. She describes it as a store of Selfridges proportions, running the length of a block with two hundred employed. 'You could buy anything and everything there. Menswear, watches, clocks, haberdashery.' She is almost lyrical about it and sad about the contrast with Kilburn today. After five years she went to work for John Lewis in Oxford Street, and then did a stint with musician Acker Bilk for a couple of years, working as his accountant after meeting him in a small hotel in Kilburn where she was the receptionist. But they didn't see 'eye to eye' and she retired after that.

Marie is always busy, yet it's as if her heart is not really in England. Whenever we talk we always talk about Ireland, about the town of Skibbereen in West Cork where she was born and returns to, two or three times a year. She shows me photographs of a trip she made last year with her friend Michael, who was recuperating from a serious operation. The pictures show them in a fishing boat, in the dining-room of the West Cork hotel, squinting in the sun outside a pub. There is one photo of Michael, standing on the river bank, pointing his way out of the frame. He is a man with what used to be called 'matinée idol' looks. Like Stewart Grainger or somebody. Silvery-haired, vigorous bright smile. She liked that last picture so much he had it enlarged and framed for her, and it is now up on her living-room wall, the country setting incongruous in a Kilburn back road. She is obviously pleased with the tribute he wrote to Skibbereen in particular, and West Cork in general, in a letter to the County Cork *Chronicle* and reproduced in the first ever edition of the Kilburn Irish Pensioners' Group magazine. He writes, 'Everywhere one looks is picture post-card scenery and is living proof that there are, in fact, forty shades of green.'

'Yes,' she nods, 'forty shades of green. It's true. You must go there.'

A devout Catholic, she goes to mass every morning and is proud of her church, the Sacred Heart in Quex Road, the largest Roman Catholic parish in England next to Westminster Cathedral. The church has two masses daily and eight masses on a Sunday. 'There are 12,000 people in that church every Sunday. It used to be 15,000.' She belongs to the Church Women's League which has fifty members: they visit the sick and the old, taking them something, a little bit of a present, doing their shopping for them. But what she seems to enjoy most is the Irish Pensioners' Group, of which she is treasurer. She shows me a picture of that, too: herself at the head of a horseshoe arrangement of tables, a small smile, sitting next to Michael who is the Chair. Most of the thirty-two counties are represented among the membership. They organise bingo and coach outings and quizzes and play Consequences, and at Christmas and St Patrick's Day they have dances, sometimes in the Quex Road Church hall. They also have discussions on topics that interest or worry them: making a will, free travel for pensioners, the poll tax.

'How are you doing for the poll tax?' she asks me. The answer is, the same as her. In a borough like Brent where the rates were high anyway, the poll tax can only benefit those with less in the house. I'm paying £498 instead of £900. She thinks the poll tax is unjust but that there is something fair in the principle that the more of you there are, the more you pay. Why should she pay the same amount of rates, for her water or her dustbins, as a house where there are ten in it? There are houses like that in our road, where the rooms are rented out to young and old men, their dustbin recesses always crowded up with their rubbish. Why does nobody clean our street? Or the High Road? Marie remembers when the street was cleaned three times a week and the High Road was swept and washed every day.

*

Kilburn Times, lead report, Thursday 8 February 1990:

AREA SHAMED BY KIDS' EYE-VIEW OF SQUALOR

Kilburn is filthy, smelly and full of muggers, tramps, dis-carded syringes and rubbish. That is how children see their local environment and, according to a child psychotherapist, it could have a serious effect on the way they grow up.

John Woods, a child psychotherapist in Brent, said a filthy environment was a breeding ground for destructive attitudes in children.

He said, 'If they are surrounded by squalor they get the message that the world can be treated as a rubbish tip and society does not care. Some will grow up to dump rubbish in the streets and drop litter.'

The shocking child's eye-view of Kilburn was revealed when children at Mazenod junior school in Mazenod Avenue, Kilburn, were asked to do a project on their local environment. The poems they wrote dealt with fights in traffic jams, broken glass, 'drug needles' and piles of stinking rubbish.

One 9 year old wrote: 'I was in Kilburn, a dirty old place. It doesn't have any fineness or grace. Rubbish piling near the sky, orange peels, gone-off eels, coke cans, lollipop sticks – anything – it was there.'

And a 10 year old spoke of 'kicking up the old tin cans along the dirty road' and 'litter bugs dropping their packets and cartons, bins overflowing, blowing pieces in the wind.'

*

Late morning, late February. A brilliantly sunny morning. The weather is mad this 1990 year, hail and wind and sunshine. It is as if winter proper has not appeared and never will now.

Kilburn Square nursery is a social-services nursery, for the poorest families in Brent, mainly single parents. It is based in a warm set of rooms in a block of maisonettes, adjacent to the fifteen-storey tower block that overlooks the Square. Pam is waiting for me in a large room full of children and toys and easels and cots. One child clings to her legs; he doesn't want to let her go. She is the kind of woman in whose presence you immediately feel stability, confidence, an innate sense of balance. She makes me a cup of tea and we take it to a large empty room that is almost all window down one side and feels cold as if the wind is coming in somewhere but you can't feel from where exactly.

She tells me she is from Blyth, Northumberland, a fishing port seven miles from Whitley Bay. Her aunt lived in Kilburn and she would come down here for holidays. When she was 19 and already qualified as a nursery nurse, her aunt sent up a notice from the local paper of jobs available in Brent. She came down for the interview without really thinking she was going to get the job, it was just good experience to come for an interview. But she did. Her mum, who had been shopping up the Kilburn High Road, burst into tears when she realised that 1 April, her start day, was only two weeks away. That was ten years ago. In the early years, the emphasis in the nursery was on the health side of things, everything had to be spick and span. '"Have you damp dusted?" they used to ask me.' Things changed dramatically around the middle of 1988, when the first round of cuts were made by Brent Council under Merle Amory, who subsequently resigned. At the end of that year, the beginning of the next, they closed seven of the fifteen nurseries in the borough. Kilburn Square was saved, but it had to take seven extra children from the closed-down places. 'I feel lucky about here. Some nurseries were being closed on health grounds. They'd found cockroaches. Others because they were pre-fab buildings. At least we couldn't be physically shut down, with fifteen floors above us. But there was a lot of anger among the girls, the girls were mad. No one could get motivated during that period. No one wanted to do anything with the children. It took a long time for us to pick ourselves up.'

Even without the immediate threat of closure, money is always the problem. Pam says, 'They try and save money, the council, by not decorating and then it comes to a point when they can't just come in and redecorate. They have to rub the whole thing down and replaster.' The problem has become structural. The room we are sitting in, that is becoming colder as we sit, had to be vacated two weeks ago because of the storm. The windows were never fitted properly anyway. It will cost £49,000 worth of work, so it is going to have to go through committee.

I ask her to describe a day at the nursery to me:

The doors open at 8 o'clock and there are children waiting. If they are hungry they'll have breakfast. Children who come in at 8 o'clock are usually quite sleepy. 'They've been dragged up and dragged out and dragged in.' If they are thirsty they'll have tea. The staff try to encourage them not to bring in bags of crisps and biscuits, so what they have is a sweety tin and everyone puts a sweety in the sweety tin and then they share it out. This encourages the children to share. By 9.30 everyone is usually in. The nursery doesn't have a policy of locking the door at a certain time. Years ago, they used to. 'IF YOU ARE NOT IN BY 10 O'CLOCK THE DOOR WILL BE LOCKED.' Pam capitalises her meaning to convey the bullying of harassed mums. 'Obviously, there are mums with two children or more maybe, under 5, who just can't get ready in time, and we don't want to be in that position of saying, you can't bring your children.'

The only time that I think about politics during a conversation where the council, money, race policy, and the social services are mentioned, is when Pam mentions food. Lunch is at 12 o'clock she says. They have Muslim and Hindu children and children who are vegetarian. Yesterday they had salad. Some had ham salad, some had cheese salad, some had egg salad. 'The children always know why each of them is having what they are having and someone else is having something different. Right from an early age we explain to them why they have this and why they don't have that. Also, there are lots of specifications on medical grounds, a lot of the children have eczema.'

She is like all the best experts: an enthusiast, allying the most concrete of knowledge with the most abstract of assertions. 'It is all so that the children feel good about themselves, about who and what they are.' The children as individuals: the child who holds on to her leg and won't let go; the child whose mum arrives late and upset and puts cut-down stockings on the child for socks. But it is also about an 'ethnic minority' policy. Everything she and the other workers do in the nursery is part of Brent's policy: it is written down somewhere. And it is, too, one of the reasons why that council, and many other Labour councils, have been so maligned. Pam knows that and she will defend the council. But she does not defend them ideologically because that doesn't make sense. I realise that for her it is not a 'race policy' at all. For her, discussing the content of each and every one's lunch with a group of 3 and 4 year olds is only about the specific implementation of proper individual care. It's only about doing her job.

When I am leaving, we go back into the room where the

children are about to have lunch. All these small people tucked under foot-high wooden tables, with huge hungry eyes. Pam introduces each of them to me by name and leads them in a chant of 'Goodbye, Melissa' when I leave. The sing-song obedience of children who don't know you. Empty of meaning but full of good will.

✳

In one sense, you can get whatever you need in Kilburn. It is a place of supreme practicality. Fresh flowers. Root vegetables. All and every kind of alcohol. Indian spices. Irish cigarettes. Arab newspapers. Old furniture. Other people's clothes, books, vases, shoes. (In the last two years, the number of charity shops on the High Road has trebled.) The 600 yards from Biddy Mulligan's pub to Lloyds Bank offers electrical goods, motor insurance, fresh fish, two off-licences, two kebab and one Greek restaurant, a pub, a funeral parlour, a musical instrument store, the Tricycle Theatre, two newsagents and stationers, a post office, a butcher, shoes again, a hardware shop. Yet if there is one consistent comment made about the Kilburn High Road by people who live in Kilburn, it is that you can't get anything on it, not anything nice. Old timers remember when you could get a good men's suit and real silk. Most major shops in London used to have a branch in Kilburn – Collins and Burton's men's outfitters, the Grange Furniture Store, Lyons Tea House, the London Co-operative. Their equivalents today are conspicuously absent; there is no branch of Next, no Habitat, no up-market tea shops. Only Woolworths and Marks and Spencer remain.

Even Kilburn's supermarkets say something about the area and its lack of economic investment. With their narrow, peeling, lino'd aisles, their shabby tills and Dynamo-tape name tags pinned to brown-check uniforms, most of Kilburn's supermarkets look provincial, now hopelessly old-fashioned compared to the cathedral of the newly opened Sainsburys supermarket set on the canal down towards Ladbroke Grove. Here, customers lucky enough to have a car, can cruise into the massive car park, walk a short distance to a building the size of an aircraft hangar, take money out from the cashpoints situated in the vestibule and then push their trolleys along aisles wide enough for two double-buggies abreast. The floor is Flash advert shining; the shelves continuously restocked. At the check-out, the girl – for it is always a she – passes each item under an electronic eye; the total is then signalled up on a screen above the cash storage box. Customers don't have to write out their own cheques: they need simply sign them. Compare this to the check-out points in Kilburn where the girl – for she always is, here too – pushes out the price of each individual item on an old style till. When she wants to know the price of an item, she presses a buzzer which calls a floating member of staff to her till who will then run to the shelf to check the price and bellow it back down the aisles. No one packs your shopping for you in Kilburn.

All that these supermarkets have in common is their overwhelming use of young, black, female labour.

*

Every day at about 4 o'clock, a group of men, mostly dressed in ragged greys and blacks, gather on the steps leading up to the hall of the Church of the Sacred Heart in Quex Road. Here, sisters of Mother Theresa's order, the Missionaries of Charity, run a soup kitchen. There is a hot meal every day, clothes provided and a bath on Thursdays. Mother Theresa's Missionaries have set up similar soup kitchens in Liverpool, Manchester and Cardiff and are now moving operations on to the Continent, to West Germany, Holland and Belgium.

Sometimes the men stand talking on the narrow pavement of Quex Road, opposite a small municipal park with a playground for children; tyres hanging from ropes on trees, some swings and roundabouts, some shrubs, but it has an empty feel, just a little bit desolate. An older man sits on a bench by the 28 bus stop, opens up a hardback book, smooths down the pages and begins to read. A couple of men are talking, cans in hand, although the strictest rule of the Missionaries of Charity is no drink. There is a bouncer in a greyish anorak to enforce the rule. He stands on the door. I watch him as the men file in; his glance shoots back and forth like secret-service professionals attached to American presidents. He radiates the suspicion of those who are hired to protect. The glance is hard and quick but it is perhaps over-professionalised. He is looking and not seeing, at one and the same time.

✳

Early on a cold Monday evening in April, Peter Pendsay comes to my house to talk to me for this piece. Afterwards, he is to go out canvassing, for the local elections in May, for Labour. He has been a councillor for Kilburn ward since 1979 and was reselected by a large majority to stand again this time. He is what he himself would call a 'serious' councillor; that is, he fulfils the nearly impossible duties of the post: attending all council, council committee and special meetings; attending to the mainly insoluble problems of constituents; and then there are the myriad get-togethers of the inner Labour Party, from the ward through to the General Management Committee to the Local Government Committee to the Labour Group of Brent Council, where Labour have a majority of twenty. Pendsay is matter of fact about the fact that it is an impossible job. 'It is social-workers' work without the social-workers' pay, impossible if you have a family life.'

Peter Pendsay was born in Baroda in Bombay Province. In 1949 he came to Britain as a staff member of Reuters news agency in Bombay. He has lived in Kilburn on and off since that time and has 'seen a lot of changes, a lot of them for the worse. It has got more dirty, crowded, overcrowded. You notice the antisocial behaviour of people, dropping litter on the street, dumping furniture.' It is the same with the rise in petty crime and muggings. He sees it 'as a symptom of the general *malaise* that the British suffer from today.'

Like many people in politics – particularly local politics, which has such a strong practical function – Peter Pendsay does not talk the ideological language of belief as much as the pragmatic language of day to day life. His constituents' main problem is housing, particularly the system of housing benefits which is so complex that no one can understand it. Many tenants are shown as in arrears when they're not. Another case he is now dealing with concerns a mother with three children living in a one-bedroom flat on the eighth floor of Kilburn Square block – up above the nursery. She applied for a transfer five years ago but has got nowhere with it. She would need to be disabled to get priority rating. Then, there are repairs. Council tenants of up to ten years have had repairs outstanding for five – water leaking through their roofs, cracks in the ceiling. 'Quite honestly, the problem has gone beyond the resources of the council. I anticipated this eight years ago. At that time I said to the Chair of Housing the situation will be reached when we, the council, will not be able to deal with housing repairs. What we should do is encourage tenants to carry out their own repairs and give them the money to do it. But it was never done and we've now reached crisis point.'

When we talk about race and racism, he says carefully that it was not a problem he personally experienced much when he first came to Kilburn and looked for somewhere to live. But, yes, there are attacks; yes, there is discrimination in housing. 'The Irish community who came here in the forties must have suffered the same way as the Asians and Afro-Caribbeans who came here in the 1960s. I'm sure many of the Irish couldn't get rooms. Kilburn does have this element – it's another symptom of the country. That's one field where Brent Council has done a lot, in housing and social services and education. Some people say the council has gone to the extreme, spending so much money on multi-cultural literature and so on. But that is the policy of the council to which it is committed; combating racism, equal opportunities, carrying on propaganda continuously.' He uses the word 'propaganda' completely unprovocatively; I am still surprised at his use of it. His fear is that there will now be cuts in race-relations' work because of the government's 'community charge' capping, announced just last week. The government say the council must cut £7,600,000 from its budget, a 'budget already cut to the bone.'

He thinks the Labour Party will win this coming May local election, with a reduced majority. The change has come only in the last week, with the poll-tax riot in Trafalgar Square. No one mentions anything but the poll tax on the doorsteps. They blame the government; it is not succeeding in its propaganda war with Labour councils.

About an hour after he leaves there is a knock on my door. Two smart professional-looking people in their early thirties are canvassing for the Labour Party. As a member of the party, my vote is secure. They move on to the next house. In appearance they remind me of pre-Steele Liberals or American Democrats. Polished but not eager, and more than a little detached. I wouldn't fancy an argument with these crisp individuals with their clipboards. They remind me, too, of something Peter Pendsay says about the change in the Labour Party, in Brent and in London as a whole: the transformation to an almost completely white-collar party. Most Labour-Party members in Kilburn are now professionals: social workers, teachers, senior council officers. There are few working-class members of the party or on the council, fewer working-class blacks. In class composition the Labour Party is now quite separate from the community it claims to represent.

*

There are no more decent cinemas in Kilburn. There used to be three. Peter Pendsay remembers when Kilburn was a place to come at night and you could dance at the State. This is going way back. The State was once the second largest cinema in Europe; Gracie Fields sang at its opening in 1926. It has preserved still its magnificent art deco entrance hall, with a Hollywood sweeping staircase and marble pillars. Now it is used for bingo, although there's a small broken-down cinema at its back, entrance in Willesden Lane. This week it's showing *Look Who's Talking* – Bruce Willis as a talking baby.

*

CLUE TO CHINESE CHEF MURDER

Police have found the trilby hat retired Chinese chef Chan Fai Leung was wearing when he was attacked and murdered thirteen days ago.

It was found in a litter bin attached to a lamp post in

Messina Avenue, Kilburn. Police are appealing for the person who put the hat in the bin to come forward. They believe the yellow tweedy trilby may hold important clues to the savage killing.

Officers are also appealing for information from witnesses who have seen Mr Leung collapse on a flowerbed at the junction of Kingsgate Road and Smyrna Road, Kilburn, about midnight on Saturday 27 January. Mr Leung was beaten to death as he walked home after celebrating the Chinese New Year. He lived in Mary Green House, Abbey Road, West Hampstead, and had been visiting friends at a Chinese restaurant in Willesden.

Somewhere between Willesden and his home he was attacked, kicked and punched in the head, and robbed. He staggered home but died the following day in hospital.

*

A savage killing.

Spike Lee's film *Do the Right Thing* took as its structure a day in the life of a network of streets in Bedford Stuyvesant, New York. It lulled the watcher into a sense of the immutability of everyday life, the joy and pain of myriad human connections. From the outset, it banished cliché and it banished sentiment. A few of the characters were near enough all good; some were pretty bad. Most of them were like most of us, a mix of the two. One minute they drive you crazy and the next you love them and I could recognise every one from my own life; the big guy with the knuckledusters tattooed 'LOVE' and 'HATE,' and the ghetto-blaster which he turned up louder and louder whenever he was criticised; I recognised that character as the girl I worked with years before, whose increasing obstinacy was a form of high volume aggression. More directly, I recognise it in

68

two mad men who hang around Kilburn. One has a sweater just like mine: a silver-grey sweater with black swirls on it; it was available in Marks and Spencer men's departments three or four years ago. I always see it on men of early middle age. This mad guy who wears it, he walks around Kilburn shouting to himself, in pain, in fury. Or laughing. In the beginning I stepped across the road when I saw him coming: to stay on the pavement felt like asking for it. Now I walk right past and try and listen in. Today I saw him, walking through a garage forecourt, carrying a packet of rice and muttering, but I couldn't hear what. And then there is the other man, who always wears a blue baseball jacket and a jockey cap and often rides a bike. He radiates a sense of threat, especially when he's smiling. I always cross over the road, even now.

At the end of *Do the Right Thing* the neighbourhood erupts in violence – murder, arson, looting. They raze the pizza parlour to the ground. But these are not the unconvincing crowd scenes of bad political cinema, as in *Sammy and Rosie Get Laid*. This is the sad and furious resolution to a story in which you feel implicated through your knowledge of the characters, your knowledge of yourself. It works precisely because it is about individuals, not symbols. It's like the quarrels you have at home when someone loses their temper and it's about fuck all and it's about everything, deadly serious. I walk along the back streets one ordinary afternoon and I hear a series of rows inside homes, one on the top floor, one right on the ground. The bass and soprano hysteria, the fractured rhythms, the sudden risings and breaks of voice are instantly recognisable; I know it could stop right there, be over, or it could get nasty.

This sense of threat is everywhere and nowhere in the city, in Kilburn.

69

For instance, two years ago this Easter, I had my two small nephews to stay, and as is the way with children, every part of the day must be plotted out with things to do, things to offer. On Sunday morning I decided, unoriginally, to take them to the Natural History Museum because the elder, Michael, likes dinosaurs. After much getting ready we step out, as three, into the sunny street. I distinctly remember looking right and then left, thinking left means getting to the bus stop much quicker (no mean consideration with two children aged 4 and 6), but right means a tree-lined walk to a better bus stop. We turned right and got on with our day. Later, the next day, I found out from the policeman conducting house to house inquiries that if we had turned left we would have had a very good chance (down to a couple of minutes) of seeing a stabbed man running along the top of Willesden Lane. This man staggered with his wounds along to a restaurant near the top of our road. There, he died.

For instance, when I go and see Marie Sargent, we inevitably talk about going out – when do you and how do you and is it safe? Every woman knows how this conversation goes. I am shocked by her saying she never goes out at night alone. Ever. She says, you hear so much and read so much. She has decided to stop taking the *Kilburn Times* because she can't read about it any more. She tells me yet again about the girl murdered at the intersection of our road and the next one down, a few years ago; about the old woman mugged by the Derby pub for just twenty pence. She has her own stories to tell: of being followed by a man from the local park. Every time she gets to a crossing he is just standing there. Luckily for her she spots a man that she knows and he says, you go home and I'll see him off. When she gets to her door, her hand is shaking so badly she can't get the key in the lock for minutes. A few years ago she was burgled in the middle of the night. She woke up to the smell of Guinness. The burglars had cracked open a can or two in her living-room and were drinking it as they contemplated what to take. She came to the top of the landing just in time to see the men's backs disappear out of the front door.

For instance, the story of Geraldine, a young petite blonde who works in the jewellers on the High Road. This story was about a mini-cab driver who drove her down a dead-end alleyway, just past the overground on West End Lane. 'We're going down West End Lane and I said, "You've passed the road," and he said, "No, I'm going down the next one," and I said, "No, the next one's no good," and we're driving down this alleyway and it was 2.00 a.m. and I said, "What are you doing?" There was nothing there but this semi-circular storage warehouse. He just looked at me in the mirror and he wouldn't speak, and that was more terrifying, him not speaking, so I was shouting and swearing, "What are you doing?" and he said, "If you don't like it, get out." So I got out and I'm walking back up, trying to get back to West End Lane. He's travelling next to me, shouting beside me, "Hey, hey, girly, come here," and I carried on, holding my breath and it was pitch dark and it felt like it was forever.'

For instance, three friends and I are sitting in the Black Lion pub in the High Road. The place is as large as a cavern and quiet for 8 o'clock on a Saturday night. There is one other group, over in a far corner. A couple of men and a woman. Suddenly, with no warning, one of the men hits the other.

71

I don't know why, I get the impression the woman is a crucial part of it. She is both goading and discouraging of the fight. Just as quickly the barmen, dressed in white shirts and thin black ties, move in and move the lot of them out. They have spotted the fight via the large round mirrors that give them back every part of the pub from the bar. Incident over.

*

Geraldine: There's nothing to do in Kilburn on a week night. Every night in the pub there's fights, people sitting outside with cuts on their heads. I don't go to the pub every day; that would be really boring. On a Friday night I might go to the Coopers, or maybe we go up to Camden, or to a club called Jockeys that goes on till about two. From there we go out wherever. Most nights we stay up till seven, go home, have a bath and go to work. By Saturday afternoon at two, I'm slaughtered. There's been a party every Friday night since October. Last summer we went to a lot of ware-house parties. There was one in Cobbingham. There were thousands of people in a field. It was my birthday that day and it was the best thing I have ever seen in my life. It was pitch-dark, but there was the light of the lasers and you could see forms. At about five in the morning it started to rain and that was really good. All the lasers made all the rain-drops a different colour because it was night-time; all these different coloured rain-drops were falling on you, it was amazing. We went there at 3.00 a.m. and we didn't get home till two the next day. I felt like a real old hippie.

*

Night sounds.

When I lived in the basement in Victoria Road, my bed was right up against the front window. So when someone was walking along my street, it was like they were walking right past my head. I used to wonder why it was everybody chose to spit right outside our window. Every time I heard it, the scraping up of the phlegm in the back of the throat and the splat on the pavement, I'd think; why right here? I worked it out. It was because people were holding it in until they turned the corner from the High Road and got into a bit of dark street.

Where I live now, it is almost back-street quiet. Easy to overhear fragments of conversation; the low drunken voices are crystal clear:

'She's a fucking slag she is.'

'She doesn't know what to do with herself.'

'She's just looking for a screw.'

All the sss's of it, like trees whispering. Then, laughter.

Deep in the night, I will be wakened very suddenly. There is a primitive roaring up on Willesden Lane, what sounds like gangs of men rampaging; then the sound of breaking glass or bins crashing; then the wail of a siren or a hurt woman. A year ago I was woken by an utterly clear, anguished cry. The voice is Irish, male, middle-aged. 'Go on, kill me then.' He spoke with such conviction. The sound of kicking. Like a detective or a cat I move from the bed to the window in two seconds and then, as often happens, I cannot see a thing. The pavement is clear but the noise is still there. The shout again. 'Go on, kill me now, you fucking bastards.' The voice cracks on 'bastards'.

This often happens too. I go to ring the police or get my friend. We will pull on our coats and go outside, face the threat. We will not be city people clutching at our nighties and dressing-gowns behind curtains. And then the noise

73

stops. It tails away, becomes a murmuring story in another street. I go back to bed, relieved.

*

With thanks to Liz and Lil Mahoney for phone numbers and insights to all interviewed here, for their time and patience; and to Paul Gordon who lived with every sentence.

Unbecoming Amateurism

MICHELENE WANDOR

I've done it. I've transgressed. I've sinned. I've committed the unspeakable. I've offended against all that is held most British and holy. What? Oh yes. I've crossed the divide from amateur to professional. Skeletons have jumped out of cupboards, devils have crawled out from beneath paper doilies, I have grown horns, claws, and I am quite clearly the most tainted and unnatural being ever to have dared to dabble in the arts.

Imagery over. What (in brief) has happened is that after some years of increasingly enthusiastic amateur music-playing and involvement with the music of the Renaissance and Baroque periods, I decided to try and go to music college and do the thing properly. This, you understand, is in addition to, not instead of being a writer. Or not even exactly 'in addition'; alongside, as an extension of, in dialectical relationship with.

It was not an easy decision. I have never had any formal music training (though I had begun to have lessons with an extraordinarily good teacher), and most of what I had done and learnt had come through the energetic enterprise of a keen amateur musician, who organises music courses for amateurs. At these I have encountered an art and people very different from many of my preoccupations of the past twenty years.

Through these courses and a network of informal contacts, I have had a very intense and rewarding involvement (as participant) in the amateur cultural movement that flourishes in this country. I know quite a lot about the amateur dramatic society movement, which keeps the publishers Samuel French in comfortable royalty percentages. I know also about the extraordinary adult-education movement which has continued in the twentieth century as an extension of working-class (and growing middling class) desire for education, self-improvement, and involvement in the whole of our cultural heritage. These are phenomena which give thousands immense pleasure, and keep alive the spirit of curiosity and inquiry which is in us all, and which (as we all know) doesn't stop with the end of formal education.

I went to classes at Morley College, and there began to play small-scale chamber music, with a self-taught finger-facility and an instinct that was reasonably good. Throughout my childhood and adult life to date this had been a relatively closet activity. Playing the recorder was (and often still is) seen as something that led on to other things. I did the expected and had a go at the flute and the clarinet, but always went back to the recorder. I didn't play any music for well over a decade, when I got married and had kids, and then, when my youngest decided he wanted to be a rock star (he isn't yet, but that's another story), I went back to my music, and that's when it all started again.

The amateurs with whom I've played come from a fairly predictable social bracket – among them are a lot of civil servants, teachers and the occasional maverick like myself. The professional tutors who give their time to work with amateurs are musicians who get something out of that overlap; amateurs may be technically unskilled, but they are usually keen and receptive, appreciative and committed. They are often people who are also the staple of the concert-going public, people who know the music from both sides as it were.

But just as there are valuable overlaps between amateur and professional, so there are very real divides, occasions when tremors can threaten the very security which makes amateur music-making such a lifeline and a pleasure for so many people. I don't as yet entirely understand what particular set of devils I have unleashed, but it feels rather serious. It is also amusing, silly and ideologically fascinating.

I took the plunge because I was unhappy with the way I was playing, and because I had ambitions for my playing. I thought I was probably nuts (my kids constantly tell me I am), but I also thought that either I was going to learn how to do it properly, or give it up. Ah. 'Do it properly.' 'Enjoy it. That's the main thing,' say amateurs of my acquaintance. Of course, that means enjoy what you can do, treat music as a social art as much as a performance for your own pleasure; don't judge yourself on the quality of the product, but on how much you enjoy the experience. But more and more I began to feel that it could (and often did) mean only play so long as you never stretch or challenge yourself; don't be seen to be too keen or too eager to improve, and don't show off. Someone I know even believes that it's wrong for music to be a profession, that it should only be something that people do for pleasure and for each other.

And here something very peculiar happens. I am thrown back to my journey through the 1970s, and the cultural legacies of the radical movements of the time: people who resurrected an early nineteenth-century utopianism in their disapproval of the cash nexus, who believed that anything that was 'professional' or defined as 'work' (class differences here) was therefore bad. It wasn't just the fact that such activity entered the commercial market-place, but that it was organised by hostile bourgeois forces (so the thinking went) into oppressive, hierarchical structures. Here an interesting elision took place between the concept of 'hierarchy' and the concept of 'structure'. The former necessarily involved the exploitation of those at the bottom of the social pile, and somehow the alternative to that was conceived as a sort of liberal utopian anarchy in which people miraculously discovered the best in themselves, and found a democratic way to work and be together which meant everyone could have a voice and a share and make a contribution.

As those of us who were involved in any of those libertarian cultural and political 'structures' know, a refusal to adhere to hierarchy did not necessarily mean an absence of structure; it simply meant that the structure went underground. Immanent privilege worked immanently; people who already were articulate and powerful continued to be so, but in concealed and covert ways. An anti-structure ideology implied a refusal to develop explicit structures through which to develop other ways of being. It seems to me that part of the reason why the radical movements failed to take adequate root was because the best aspects of responsible professionalism were thrown out with the bathwater. People talked about accountability but were not interested in exploring ways in which accountability could work. Feminism was as guilty of this as socialism. By the time the 1980s discovered the delights of the concept of structure (through the intellectual exploits of academics who took up structuralism and its twin, deconstruction), and by the time the 'professionalised' left began to appear in local govern-

Grandma and granddaughters, London, 1987.

Nuns of St Petersbourne, London, 1983.

Seasonal workers, Llandudno, 1986.

Pit brew lasses, Wigan, 1983.

Day-trippers, Isle of Sheppey, 1987.

Council tenants, London, 1986.

Single parent, London, 1983.

Disco-goers, Hillingdon, 1982.

ment, the ideals of the early, libertarian, and essentially amateur movements had faded and become muddied by the destructiveness of the apparently structureless.

Of course, there is no crude parallel between the amateur music movement and the radical political movements of the 1960s and 1970s; but both owe a contradictory allegiance to the wonderful and exasperating spirit of British amateurism, and somehow, in my decision of a year ago, I tripped and fell straight into that chasm of contradiction. When I told music-playing friends that I was going to become a full-time music student, I met with a curious set of reactions. A very small number were curious, interested in why, and supportive. A larger number were curious, critically inquiring (the 'Why on earth are you bothering to do that?' approach) and implicitly disapproving; some were admiring that I should take the risk of laying myself on the line – after all, I might prove to be inadequate, be unable to learn, etc., – and some were downright hostile, and resentful, as if somehow I had been the recipient of some entirely undeserved privilege.

Now that I am a music student, I have to come to terms with the opposite approach; that peculiar competitive ethos of a college where people are being trained for a profession which is precarious and cut-throat. Here the simple delights of the amateur group who meet for the sheer pleasure of experiencing music together are absent. Here the tensions of learning are present. Here the egos of arts students have to cope with the contradictions of a relatively sheltered environment which is constantly encouraging them to brave their own ignorance at the same time as produce the performing goods.

Here there is an edgy alliance between tolerance and judgement; in the professional world judgement is all, and already at college the vocational pedagogic process incorporates it sufficiently to give everything an extra edge. In the amateur world, process is all, and in the professional world, product is all. In the amateur world a pleasurable process sometimes results in a genuinely qualitative work of art; in the professional world the product is sometimes preceded by a genuinely pleasurable process. Having complained about those who have implied criticism of my desire to shift from amateur to professional, I sometimes have the sneaky feeling that my desire for pleasurable process and quality product is itself a sixties utopian hangover. I am one of the most cynical people I know, and yet I still want what seems to be rarely possible.

It ought to be possible to be responsible, accountable, fair, supportive and enabling; it would be nice to implement professional approaches to process, whether the context is amateur or professional. The amateur environments which work best are those which are organised in a structured way that gives all abilities a chance, and that involves a high degree of organisational nous and understanding – professionalism, in a word. That's why Britain has a tradition of flourishing, active amateurism; if some of the ease and generosity of amateurism were applied to the professional world, and if some real recognition of the value of professionalism were allowed into the amateur ethos, we might have more of a continuum and less of a divide. And both politics and art might be the richer for it.

The Personal Politics of Ageing

MARY STOTT

'The personal is political', we of the women's liberation movement said in the sixties-into-seventies. It is just as true of the experience of the elderly and aged in the nineties. You cannot talk effectively about old age without being political – analysing how society treats its older citizens – and you should not talk about old age without drawing on the personal experience of ageing. So this contribution to *Storia* is inescapably bifocal.

Looking first through the long-distance lens: One must begin by listing society's obligations to those who have reached retirement age, and how it fulfils them. First and foremost: Since Lloyd George introduced the old-age pension in 1911, society has accepted responsibility for basic maintenance for those unable any longer to earn their own living. In present-day terms, this pension should cover the cost of a place to live and of food to eat, but also the cost of keeping that home warm and lighted and of cooking the food. As I write, the basic pension for a single person is £46.90. Is that sufficient to cover these basic needs, plus a small margin for clothes, etc? Many of us would doubt it.

At least the great majority of old people still live in homes they own, by now mortgage-free, or in homes rented from their local authority. I doubt whether those who reach retirement age after the turn of the century will be able to say as much, for local authorities have been encouraged to sell off their houses to sitting tenants and have by no means replenished their housing stock. (In the 1960s local authorities built an average of 152,000 houses a year. In 1988 the number had dropped to 21,000.)

The amount of 'sheltered housing' available for those who find home maintenance a problem is also lessening. Around the country there are still admirable council-owned housing projects which offer a sitting-room, bedroom, kitchen and bathroom at a modest rent to senior citizens, with a resident warden to keep an eye on all the tenants; but few if any are being built now, and residential accommodation for the elderly is passing into the hands of private entrepreneurs who almost all charge prohibitive rents and some of whom permit their staff to ill-treat and bully their tenants. Is this decline due to the fact that our 'caring' government takes the view that the elderly are better off in the homes of their sons and daughters and their spouses? I often ask myself how Mrs Thatcher would like to have to ask for bed and board in the home of her daughter.

Back to the financial aspect of living in your own home: You have, of course, to pay poll tax (which in the case of single persons may perhaps be less than the previous rates demand). You also have to pay for water, gas and electricity, and the standing charge will be the same for you as for a family of five or six who consume a great deal more than a single person. In the case of British Telecom the standing charge plus VAT is much higher. In my case the standing charge plus VAT just about equals the charge for outgoing calls. That is absurd, grossly unfair, and a matter that is certainly as much political as personal. Elderly people living alone need the telephone as a lifeline to summon help in the event of an accident or sudden illness, such as a heart attack. It has often occurred to me that if we really had a Welfare State the best way to ensure that aged persons could avoid the risk of hypothermia in freezing winters would be to provide fuel coupons along with the pension books during the winter months, which the recipients could use to pay their gas, electricity or coal bills.

The second vital responsibility society has undertaken towards its elderly members is health care; this dates back to the passing of the National Assistance Act in 1945, and may be regarded as the emergence of the Welfare State. The Act ensured free medical treatment for all, and free prescriptions for children and the elderly. This provision too has deteriorated alarmingly in the 1980s. A personal experience will illustrate this fact. In 1989 I became aware that my sight had deteriorated and that I almost certainly needed new lenses. I booked an appointment at the local optician's and presented myself at the desk on the due date. Having checked my particulars the receptionist said, 'I am afraid I shall have to ask you for £10.50 before I can let you through to see the oculist.' Outrage almost choked me. I have been having eye tests since I was 11 years old (when presumably my father paid a fee to the eye specialist as well as paying for the lenses and frames, as there was no National Health Service then). In my more affluent days, always rather anxious to safeguard my sight, I also paid a specialist's fee, but when I decided that examination by the oculist on duty at the local optician's premises was probably adequate, there was no charge for examination, any more than there would be at one's family doctor . . . until 1989.

My outrage was caused by the fact that I well know that eye tests are an aspect of *medical* examination. They are the only way that a serious eye defect, leading to glaucoma and perhaps to blindness, can be discerned. Spectacles are not simply a convenience for easier reading. They are, for many ageing people, a life-protecting necessity (as in crossing the road).

But of course I made out my cheque for £10.50, which I can afford to pay, having small earnings, a small occupational pension and a small investment income on top of my state pension. But supposing my *only* income had been the state pension of £46 – how could I then have afforded it? Should I not have shrugged my shoulders and walked away muttering to myself, 'Well I suppose I shall have to manage'? That, in fact, is what a great many people must have done after this eye test charge was imposed for adults of all ages in April 1989, for in the next few months the number of people taking eye tests dropped by 40%. Up to the time of writing we pensioners have not only free access to our family doctors, but free prescriptions. Can we be sure that this will continue?

Of course, pensioners can apply for Social Security aid. But why should we impoverished old have to *ask* for help? In June 1989, during a House of Lords' debate on child benefit, Lady Jeger told the story of 'a very respectable man' who declared that never again was he going to apply for family benefit because he had been required to disclose all his financial affairs 'over the counter to a bit of a girl.' Lord Seebohm enlarged on that: 'Many people find it humiliating to go with a begging bowl to talk to a clerk and stand naked in all their affairs . . . A great many people feel so humiliated by this that they will not do it.'

Reading this debate I was slightly surprised to find that

the speaker with whom I empathised was a Conservative hereditary peer, Lady Strange, who said: 'Child benefit is received by all, like the rain, falling on the just and the unjust; those who need it and those who do not. We pride ourselves on being a caring society. Let us vote for continued child benefit which, like the well-advertised lager, reaches the parts that other benefits cannot reach.'

'Targeting' is the current 'in' word for social benefits. To those of us who remember the Depression of the early thirties, 'targeting' is just a euphemism for 'means-testing', and no one who recalls Walter Greenwood's famous novel *Love on the Dole* can ever endure the idea of means-testing as social policy.

In no area is the political more personal than in the effect of inflation, for it discriminates against the really old in a way that few younger people understand. Few people who retired in the early seventies, before inflation took off (other than civil servants, teachers and employees of local authorities) had an index-linked occupational pension. And in those years a very acceptable salary for an experienced professional employee might well be no more than £3,000 a year – a ludicrously small sum by today's standards. A pension based on this salary amounts to no more than £140 a month. Moreover, those people who had managed to make fairly substantial savings to cushion their old age have found them devalued too. Is it surprising that one feels indignant that clever young journalists should write about the enviable lifestyle of the 'golden oldies'?

This seems the point at which an examination of the personal should take over from the political. The lower half of the bifocal lenses can reveal a problem seldom recognised by younger people. It is psychological, not factual. We can remember the penny post, so we grimace when the cost of stamps for Christmas cards and presents takes up practically all that £10 Christmas bonus a munificent government hands out to pensioners. It is not funny to discover that we simply cannot afford to be as lavish in our Christmas-present buying as our nears and dears, even our young grand-children.

Looking through treasured souvenirs of earlier days we may come upon a little brochure of a fabulous pre-war holiday. Yes, fabulous – 23 guineas for an 'Italian train cruise' lasting fourteen days which took in Stresa, Milan, Venice, Florence, Naples, Rome. One's salary at that time was probably about £7 a week – but relative values are very difficult to work out. That splendid old Jaeger top coat lurking in the back of the wardrobe, bought for £25 in the early sixties, would be at least £250 now, and what younger people find almost impossible to understand is that even if one could afford such a sum one *would* not because it would seem appalling extravagance.

The crippling effect memories of pre-inflation prices have on our spending extends to essentials as well as to 'luxuries'. To food, for example. To spend more than a pound or so on the main ingredient of a main meal seems quite unwarranted extravagance; to spend more than £10 a head on a restaurant meal seems quite disgraceful. Trying to explain the psycho-logical effect of inflation on our spending is a plea for under-standing, not sympathy. One does not *need*, for example, to spend £250 on a top coat. One can take great pleasure in one's clothes if they are bought from Oxfam or other charity shops, or from sales at the local Friends Meeting House, especially if you are the sort of person who takes pleasure in 'mixing and matching' – shirts, skirts, jumpers, trousers and so on. Youngsters may find it humiliating to wear other people's cast-offs, but few pensioners do – or have any need to. Because we pay less we can have more choice!

In fact the personal view of the first few months of the winter of ageing is a great deal less bleak than the view of the outsider looking in. The 60- to 70-year-olds – the 'young old' as they have been called – are not a problem. They are, or should be considered, a resource. They should be recruited – and recruit themselves – into all kinds of public activity. We may not care very much for the policies of our Prime Minister, but she is an outstanding proof that a woman of pensionable age can have the brains, the energy and the determination to run a country. It is a shocking waste of brains and experience that the newly retired, especially women, are not more often recruited to public bodies and commissions. Think of all the retired headmistresses, matrons, civil servants and local authority department heads who are available! There must be something very wrong with our present appointments' system that so few of them are recruited to serve.

But if one is not asked, one can still give. There are countless causes one can support. (There were plenty of grannies at Greenham.) Or one can initiate one's own campaign, like that remarkable woman Ollie Hollingsworth, who was a fitter's mate on the railway during the Second World War. In her later years quite small things set her campaigning, like the dangerous cracks in pavements and kerbs, and the difficulty in buying very small portions of meat and fish, etc. She got together a handful of like-minded men and women and formed Tooting Action for Pensioners, which campaigned with remarkable vigour to help the aged in various fields. Ollie was twice threatened with being thrown out of a local council meeting.

Of all the activities that keep the ageing person in good

bodily and mental health, campaigning probably is the best, for inevitably one makes new friends, most of them a good deal younger. The variety of causes is endless, from Greenpeace to pavement parking. It is hard to feel sympathy for the poor old lady who wrote in her diary every day 'Nobody came'. Why didn't *she* go out? Or, if she was too frail to venture out on her own, why didn't she *invite* people to call? It is surprising that no one seems to have set up a 'chatline' for the old and lonely. Without doubt one of the most trying things about old age is having no one to talk to; and it is especially trying for those who have spent long years in happy partnership with husband or wife.

Looking through the lower half of one's bifocals, one inevitably observes other problems which are not seen as 'political'. The basic fact is that one is conscious of wearing out. Wear out, rust out: which is worse? Wearing out may be preferable for one's lifestyle, but the result is much the same as with rusting out – a diminishing of one's power in almost every field. Another personal experience to illustrate this sad fact: I live in a Victorian house divided into flats, and have oldish equipment: a 20-year-old electric cooker and an even older twin-tub washing machine. (The house shows its age: the woodwork is beginning to crack away from the walls in places, the pipes are beginning to corrode and even the brickwork to crumble a little here and there.)

Recently a very alarming electrical fault struck our supply. A great surge of power 'blew' six light bulbs and also various items such as a music centre, and the clock, timer and auto-clean on the cooker – which was declared to be non-repairable.

This was not only a financial worry but a rather painful reminder that human 'parts' also wear out and cannot be restored to full functioning. Sight and hearing almost inevitably deteriorate with age, but sight and hearing aids are available at a price. Much more alarming, however, is a deterioration of some functions of the brain, and as far as I know there is no way of reconditioning the thinking mechanism to improve its performance. Everyone knows the difficulty older people have in remembering names or even ordinary words. It is possible sometimes to track down the right word through mnemonics of one kind or another, but I have found no way to fix events in the mind. Once I found, to my utter shame, that I had forgotten the death of the wife of an old friend, even though I had dutifully written a letter of condolence at the time. I keep a pretty detailed daily diary now – not for posterity, but simply so that I can track down events, if necessary, some weeks or months later.

This memory loss affects almost every aged person. It feels rather as if a cassette tape has been over-used and slips an inch or two. Yet, unlike the worn-out cassette, one's brain will quite often produce the right word, the right incident, a fraction of a minute later. Other times the name may not surface for hours or even days.

After too many experiences like this, one begins, in the depressing hours of a wakeful night, to fear that memory loss may indicate the onset of Alzheimer's disease, the most horrific of the degenerative diseases. Alzheimer's disease is a progressive destruction of the brain cells and may result in the victim's becoming a sort of mindless little old animal. If you have ever seen a loved friend or relation reduced to this condition you can never be entirely free from fear.

So then one begins to ask: 'In what way will this mortal coil finally be shuffled off? And how soon? And what then?' One's friends say, 'Oh, don't be morbid.' But it is not morbid. It is an elementary fact that we have to die, and possibly the best way to deal with this is to give some time to contemplation – not only to what possibilities a life beyond offers, but to what life still offers here and now. A great deal, I think, if one has a family, friends, a Cause . . . and a garden.

Pop Pastiche and the New Regeneration

LUCY O'BRIEN

TIRED AND EMOTIONAL

Pop is continually looking for the new Regeneration. A rag-bag of market trends and multifarious tribal styles, British pop is struggling with Pop Fatigue and suffering a lost innocence. In an industry that thrives on difference and in-built obsolescence, fans and performers alike are constantly searching for the next Big Thrill, whether it be the latest hardcore band or the new Madonna. Pop, after all, is about the sensation of fast turnover, counting on the pang of discovery and desire when you first hear that powerful record.

Now rivalling the film industry in its ability to attract lucrative markets, pop has been expanding throughout the eighties. No longer centred on the 7-inch single, pop is presented on movie soundtracks, adverts, video, fashion shows and sporting events. It's consumed in a variety of formats, from vinyl to tape and CD, and thoroughly mediated through the specialist music press, pop glossies like *Smash Hits*, daily papers and a wide range of youth

TV. The pop fan is bombarded with information and a bewildering morass of trends and styles. With so much history to plunder and imitate, pop seems to have lost its purity of purpose.

In order to understand the wayward proliferation of pop, it's necessary to go back. Because if one thing is certain about the eighties, it was pop's inveterate habit of looking back at other eras for influences, instant feedback or ideas. The most poignant theme to emerge was that of lost innocence, and one way to quantify that is to look at the nostalgia of my own innocence.

FLICKS AND HAIRSPRAY

Things seemed so much simpler in the seventies. Pop then was a system of certainties. At the age of 14 I had regulation cardboard flicks in my hair, stapled back with a liberal dose of hairspray. The knot in my school tie was humungous, my wedge shoes were huge, the flares on my Oxford Bags just *so*. I had a red, cap-sleeved T-shirt I was very proud of, stripy socks and cherry lip gloss. And so did all my friends.

We listened to The Sweet, Roxy Music and T. Rex, and laughed at The Glitterband, Mud and The Bay City Rollers. Later we all watched John Travolta when *Saturday Night Fever* pranced in, sweeping disco into high streets and Top Ranks across the land.

Pop was about inane certainties, as unshakeable as our platforms. 'I love you love me love', 'Tie a yellow ribbon round the old oak tree'. Even 'Chirpy chirpy cheep cheep', for God's sake. Every Sunday night I spent glued to Radio One, listening to the Top Twenty, writing down words to the songs and perfecting the latest formation dances with my friends. There was glitter on your cheek, sequins on your jumpers, and the priorities were clear: either you liked The Osmonds or David Cassidy. It was not uncommon for rival sets of fans to beat each other up, such was the commitment to their idols and the power of pop.

In the early seventies, British pop was about what Fred and Judy Vermorel would call The Girl. 'As screamager, nubie, fan, the GIRL acts out for all of us our consumerist deliriums of possession and ecstasy . . . Whether in blue jeans, bobby sox or bare legs, the GIRL is of no particular gender. You only need to be excitable, vulnerable, *fun* to be a GIRL.'[1]

Pop in the seventies was more idealistic, the demarcation lines clear with a hierarchy of influences, rather than the mass amalgam it is today. If you were a young teenager, glam pop, The Carpenters and David Essex were the gods. As you got older, there was the pull of 'mature' progressive rock with 'mature' drum solos, pompous sixth-form lyrics and vegetating hippie names like Black Sabbath, Deep Purple and Pink Floyd. And there was disco, pulsating from the margins of Black America to take over production processes throughout the industry.

Music was cleanly compartmentalised, restricted to two TV shows: *Top of the Pops* (lowbrow) and *The Old Grey Whistle Test* (highbrow). Apart from rock papers *Melody Maker*, *Sounds* and *NME*, teenage pop desires were catered for in the print medium only in the form of *Disco 45*. Forget *i-D*, *this* was the style Bible of the seventies. Each week the lyrics of your favourite hits were printed in their entirety, including the immortal phrase: 'Repeat till fade.'

LEADER OF THE GANG

Pop was the soundtrack to growing up, getting a job and wearing blue eye shadow. There were no such things as YTS or compulsory training schemes, no AIDS to threaten your sexual experimentation, less social or political pressure to make youth such a fearful and cynical complexity. Pop tribalism was restricted to the width of your flares or the height of your wedge heels. It was a bold, aggressive time, when the fashions were ugly, the poses striking. At school you *knew* who the rebels were, whether they were badly behaved or plain inspired. You knew what being a rebel meant, before punk dictated that you could be a rebel just by *looking* like one. To us the sixties seemed like a far-off dream, further off even than they are now, half-remembered as a mesh of incense, Haight Ashbury hippies and Free Love.

The seventies was about being clumpy, clumsy, vulgar and *certain*. Pop, with its reassuring Top Twenty and Radio One roadshows, confirmed the solidity of a generation safe with the Welfare State and a then reasonably funded education system. Pop ran on linear lines, Chinn and Chapman produced hundreds of hits for Smokie, Mud and Suzi Quatro, and the high point of our night at the disco was the lights turned low, a slow dance and The Chi-Lites singing: 'Church bells ringin' and the angels singin' . . . in.'

It was too secure to last. The revolution in micro-chip technology completely changed the surface structure of pop, unemployment began to decimate our young, and political absolutes were agitated by media-heavy postmodernism.

Until then music history had been unfolding at a regular pace with all the myths and received wisdom firmly in place. We were aware that the fifties had been a blast. On the one hand there was the British post-war tradition of camp show

94

tunos and family entertainment with such artists as Ruby Murray and The Beverley Sisters. On the other was the sound of rock-'n'-roll from Bill Haley to young Elvis, directly descended from the blues and mangled up with a radical beat.

Such fresh musical innovation shocked the charts over here, so that by the sixties, Britain was awash with Beat groups, taking their cue from Stateside R & B. With acts like The Beatles, Dusty Springfield, The Rolling Stones and the Dave Clark Five *reinterpreting* rather than slavishly copying American sounds, a brand new buzz was created. Britain was beginning to discover it had a teen-age, with the sheer exuberance of mods, rockers and assorted youth cults feeding the talent that paraded across to America with the first British Invasion.

By the late sixties, pop was already affecting a complex veneer, reflecting vivid counter-culture trends in the growth of moody acid-bound rock. Pop entered a self-conscious, older adolescent phase. Everything became psychedelic – from The Beatles' 'Strawberry Fields' to The Temptations in their 'Psychedelic Shack'. In the face of hippiedom, established British pop stars became unstuck. The conventional road for performers like Tom Jones and Dusty Springfield ended up being pensioned off in cabaret and summer panto-mime. British pop had to change and regenerate itself by combining the glamour and glitz of straightforward enter-tainment with the eccentric impulses of the 'avant-garde' rock world.

By 1974 the results were beginning to show, with an impish, temperamental young man called Marc Bolan. With his Medusa-like hair and glittering guitar, Bolan transfor-med the typically sixties hippie group Tyrannosaurus Rex into the decidedly seventies T. Rex, and launched a thousand screams. Who could fault the irony of songs like 'Children of the Revolution', with the words 'I drive a white Rolls-Royce/'Cos it's good for my voice'?

Alongside Bolan was David Bowie à la Ziggy Stardust. With his jagged facial stripe, body stockings and freak orange hair, Bowie was a precursor to punk. Drenched in the myths of rock-'n'-roll, he still managed to turn a guitar lick into a pop hit and himself into a teenage idol. Also pitched in the register of high glam were Roxy Music, all futurist costumes, tacky scenery and larger-than-life pop drama. With his svelte-suited appeal, their frontman, Bryan Ferry, was one of the first British designer pop stars, a triumph of chic style.

In the seventies pop came of age. Along with the flatulence of over-ripe rock groups, existing on large record company advances and hung-over sixties' drug habits, was the breezy confidence of British glam. Such ebullience was personified in the stamping figure of Noddy Holder. With his beaming face, tight braces and gigantic platforms, the lead singer (we use the term loosely) of Slade pulled out the most raucous elements of seventies' pop, as if he was extracting its teeth. Then pop was barefaced, arched and disingenuous. It mooned at you. How *could* it have the sophistication of a nineties' packaged pop group? Then the notions of stylist and designer were in their infancy. A seventies' marketing strategy was simply about getting your records in the shops.

AGITATION

Our bliss was bound to be disturbed. Lulled by Abba and The Eagles at the end of the seventies, no one foresaw pop's frantic future. The move towards uncertainty was ably assisted by the phenomenon of punk rock.

As a teenager growing up in calm Southampton, a city known for the docks, the QE2, football and very little else, I remember the shockwaves that reverberated when pockets of Sex Pistols' followers appeared on the scene. There was a memorable 'gosh look at this' article in *The Observer* about 'punk rockers . . . an alienated generation who spit and wear bin liners', featuring a picture of The Damned wearing safety-pins in their cheeks. On came my drainpipe jeans, out came the disapproval of my boy-friend. 'You're not going round with me looking like that,' he said. My friends and I worked out a way of fixing safety-pins in our cheeks without the pain. Being convent girls, we proudly formed an unapologetic all-female band called The Catholic Girls.

If the seventies were ugly, punk tried to make them uglier, rejecting flares for straight jeans, declaring anti-fashion with ripped T-shirts and bondage gear. And the music! Elvis and all those seventies rock groups were so *boring*. No one needed to be clever to play. According to Mark Perry in his Sniffin' Glue fanzine, all you needed was three chords, and then you could form a band.

The situationist tendencies of groups like The Sex Pistols, The Clash and Siouxsie and the Banshees came as an anathema to the regular seventies' generation. Punk, however, was a logical extension of seventies' glam. Tormentedly loud, it took the stomp and drama of seventies' pop, leaving out the idealism to inject a reactionary force of cynicism. For a few years British pop was under siege, overtaken on one side by the commercialism of American disco and trammelled on the other by punk's nihilistic death wish. It was pretty uncomfortable then being a record executive.

But there was light at the end of the tunnel. The original

burst of punk was brief, burning itself out by 1979. In its wake came the more respectable, user-friendly New Wave. Now bands brought up on punk were coming out with *melody lines* and *hooks* and *dance beats*. There were punk Wombling songs for the kids, too. Splodgenessabounds' 'Two Pints of Lager and a Packet of Crisps Please' played up punk's nursery attraction, as did Jilted John's 'Gordon Is a Moron' and 'We're Going Down the Pub' by Sham 69.

The longer-lasting development for eighties' pop came in the fusion of raw punk and old-style songwriting – a combination cosseted and made slick by the New-Wave Godfather, Elvis Costello. His adherence to irony predated the new generation of designer pop stars who, schooled by the cynicism of punk, applied their own self-conscious rules to the pop process. Heaven 17 drew on a whole history of British pop and American funk to make a crisp, political dance record: 'We Don't Need this Fascist Groove Thing'. Human League moved from their esoteric synth-art background into the mainstream by recruiting two girls from a Sheffield night-club, and turning themselves into a latter-day Abba.

Eurythmics, too, tuned into pop manipulation. Once laughed at as part of a run-of-the-mill power pop band called The Tourists, Dave Stewart and Annie Lennox commanded respect in 1983 when the ferocious burst of their bass synthesizer in 'Sweet Dreams' dominated the charts. There was also Lennox's look, deliberately androgynous and a 'male' counterpart to the gender confusion of Boy George and Culture Club.

The British pop resurgence of the early eighties was mainly video-led. With a long tradition of obsessive subcultural style, our pop videos exploited the visual impact of the sharp haircut, the fifties' suit, and punk-inspired dayglo wackiness. All this was suited to the nascent MTV – then a mere cable experiment in the US looking for bright new blood. In the same way that the sixties' Beat groups invaded America with their ironic sparkle, so the eighties' designer boys and girls excited US consumers by bending a few gender rules and coming up with confident soul pop.

LOST INNOCENCE

There is a fine line, though, between clever irony and cultural pastiche. It takes strong intuition and stringent observation now to come up with a pop package that is culturally cutting or vaguely original.

While the designer bands of the early eighties taught us the joy of manipulation, their very self-consciousness set pop's agenda for the rest of the decade. The Sex Pistols' crude situationism certainly uncovered the nuts and bolts of pop hype and debunked the myth of pop stardom being the natural result of natural talent, but it also paved the way for an attitude steeped in stultifying expression.

Bands preoccupied with their own artifice gradually sank into the safety of imitation. Ten years on, the once-striking white dance band ABC are now parodying *themselves* with turgid variations on their early hit 'Poison Arrow'. Culture Club, who so cleverly reinvented Tamla Motown on 'Church of the Poison Mind', then tripped over the bloated beast they had created by recording the infantile 'War Song': 'War is stupid/People are stupid', sang Boy George in all seriousness.

Eighties' pop was at the forefront of a general style revolution. What began as a shake up of entertainment and media mores became *de rigueur* as the decade wore on. Magazines like *The Face* and *i-D* that had started off as hungry, sharp and arrogant, hugely influencing mainstream design and typography, gradually settled into the house style expected of them.

Discussion about style almost displaced content – to the extent that in 1987, Cameron McVey from the carefully planned CBS pop duo Morgan McVey could say: 'The eighties is a really honest era – the sixties was an illusion. People aren't afraid of success, which is good, but also the eighties is a DIY era. All we're doing is playing the game. We're really blatant about it to the point that if the music sounds right we might change it, 'cos it doesn't fit into the genre of what we are.' After the failure of his eighties' pop band, McVey is now a prime mover (some would say Svengali) in the career of rap star Neneh Cherry.

Playing the game in the eighties and nineties has become infinitely more complex than the bang-out-a-record-and-a-bit-of-hype approach employed in previous decades. Each act now signed to a record company is surrounded by an armoury of producers, arrangers, stylists and designers, all able to customise a 'look' and a sound for a particular audience, which is then mediated by sympathetic magazine editors.

This artful self-regard permeates British pop production, cancelling out naïvety. Glasgow, one of the most creative pop cities of the eighties, is saturated in lost innocence. In transforming its own image from a working-class industrial centre to a 1990 post-industrial city of culture, the city itself threw up a whole generation of bands – Simple Minds, Deacon Blue, Hue And Cry, Texas, Love And Money – who all looked back to a previous generation or another culture (preferably American) to create a sound that according to Hue And Cry's Pat Kane 'is like reproducing your favourite records or your pal's record collection'. On their first LP 'Seduced and Abandoned', Kane even went to New York to record with James Brown's horn players and Sinatra's string section.

Fuelling this revivalism has been the resurgence of sixties' stars recording with eighties' artists in mutually beneficial duos. The Pet Shop Boys have recorded with long-term heroines Dusty Springfield and Liza Minelli, while synthmoguls The Art of Noise roped in Tom Jones to sing a camp, raunchy version of Prince's 'Kiss'. Marc Almond resuscitated Gene Pitney for an emotive reworking of his sixties' hit 'Something's Gotten Hold of My Heart', while The Smiths heart-throb Morrissey sought out sixties' pin-up Sandie Shaw to sing his song 'Hand in Glove'.

These hits went hand-in-hand with incongruous House remixes of old songs like Petula Clark's 'Downtown' or The Beatles' 'Strawberry Fields'. Alongside the retro chic of Levis' adverts, the selling of the past became a powerful commercial force. The focus now is less on achieving the classic pop song than in approximating *indicators* of pop classics. The Fine Young Cannibals are past-masters of this art, dabbling a Motown drum-beat here, or a soul melody line there to come up with a sound that proficiently reproduces shades of pop's best. The only trouble with albums like 'The Raw and the Cooked' is that they lack the charge of one unified pop song. A successful pop single should be like an argument: cogent, whole and forcefully pushing the point home.

Mike Stock, Matt Aitken and Pete Waterman (SAW) are the terrible trio of late eighties' pop production. They'd agree with the idea of pop song as argument, only theirs is driven home with cliché. SAW have their apologists who say, 'Lots of people buy their records/their artists are

101

extremely commercial/therefore they must be good.' Have any of these people listened to a Kylie record all the way through? Kylie Minogue and Jason Donovan are repetitive, diluted versions of seventies' magic. Where The Osmonds or The Bay City Rollers were brash, sickly and larger-than-life, Kylie and Jason are just sickly. Easy pastiche is used in their presentation, with Kylie sporting a sartorial mix of Top Shop chic and watered-down fifties' Marilyn Monroe.

Much is made of the 'innocence' of a SAW record. Innocence is impossible in eighties' pop and pointed proof of that can be found, ironically, in the work of SAW – so much of it based calculatedly on seventies' disco and on the back of former DJ Pete Waterman's uptempo soul collection.

From Sinitta to Rick Astley to the England Football Team, SAW records are interchangeable. They all have the same pasteurised compulsive pop beat that derives from a strain of early High Energy. Each song has a clear tune and a simple hookline: 'I should be so lucky, lucky, lucky, lucky', 'Fun, love and money', 'Never gonna give you up . . . ' These declarative statements are directed into the heart of the teenage market, and yes, lots of pubescent girls have bought it. But the bland dominance of SAW production techniques has acted like a dead weight on much late eighties pop output, making pale simulation the norm. At least Brian Connelly of The Sweet *surprised* us in 1973 when he stuttered 'Ballroom Blitz'.

THE PHUTURE

Technology has proved to be a tyrant in the making of modern pop. In the past we could count on 'real' music:

'real' guitars, 'real' voices, 'real' spontaneity. There's the amplified shuddering breaths on Dusty Springfield's 'You Don't Have To Say You Love Me', the cavernous soap tragedy of The Shangrilas' 'The Leader of the Pack', or the simple orchestrated uplift of Smokey Robinson's 'Tracks of My Tears'. There's also T. Rex's glam guitar and the keyboard sparks of Roxy Music's 'Virginia Plain'.

Now these edges are smoothed down and rounded for pristine radio play. The introduction of the digitally remastered CD in the eighties meant there was little room for difference. When SAW want a production sound, a particular bass line or a drum riff, they programme it. Phil Spector used to cram his whole orchestra into the recording studio for one tumultuous take. While there is no point in becoming a pop Luddite – musical computer technology, after all, has been with us since the seventies – it's important to recognise its uniformity of effect. In the same way that writing straight on to a word processor cuts out some necessary graft, so programming an entire pop song eradicates a degree of inspirational difficulty. The secret lies in making that technology work for you rather than letting it dictate your style.

Peter Ford, the angular young space cadet behind pop group Baby Ford, is part of a new generation of computer literate pop stars, honing the tools of technology to their own dance beat:

> The most important thing to me is getting an idea or picture together. It's like having a piece of paper and sketching out an idea, putting colour to it. I'm not a muso arty painter, I just try things out. Sometimes it turns out a little bit abstract or wrong – sometimes it's better to leave it like that, with human error. I work

with computers. I'm not a computer *kid*, but I work with a programmer. The technical stuff is your painting brush, your instrument.

The use of technological sampling and cut up beats was something pioneered by hip hop, the Stateside urban black dance music that drove tramlines through contemporary pop in the mid-eighties. While pop was drowning in the media morass of huge events like Live Aid, Band Aid and stadium rock, up popped hip hop. What began as sparse gunslinging DJ chat over a turntable beat grew into a sophisticated collage of rhythm, soundbites and loony tunes. Rap hits like Real Roxanne's 'Bang Zoom Let's Go Go' and Run DMC's 'Walk This Way' served to introduce hip hop to the mainstream.

In Britain rap developed a hybrid style all of its own, with several strands influencing rap hits by the late eighties. Firstly there was the Jamaican dance-hall influence that filtered through from the reggae sound systems set up by the first generation of black Britons.

The most successful of these has been Soul II Soul, a loose conglomeration of London artists, musicians, dancers and designers led by the self-styled millionaire of street sass, Jazzie B. In 1989 Soul II Soul records like 'Keep On Movin'' and 'Back to Life' set out a new laid-back pop philosophy of life, incorporating reggae dub beats and sweet melody lines. Jazzie's hits pilfer from a whole history of dance, but it's his ability to come up with a fusion that's new that saves Soul II Soul from the clutches of mere pastiche.

Another strand tunnelling into British pop via the techniques of hip hop was disco, or its latter-day equivalent, House music. A relatively unimportant figure in the seventies, the club DJ has been deified in late eighties' pop. It has long been common practice for DJs in clubs to mix and match different dance records to come up with a challenging beat. This effect was committed to vinyl in 1986 with MARRS' massive dance hit 'Pump Up the Volume', a track that segued extracts from a multitude of top dance numbers. Not deeming it a serious pop contender, Radio One had refused to play it, but through sheer force of its popularity in the clubs the record became a No. 1 hit. In its wake followed a host of Stars-On-45 type copyists, mixing to fever pitch.

The next big British disco record was 'The Theme from S-Express', concocted by London nighthawk and established DJ Mark Moore. The fact that it went straight to No. 1 totally flummoxed him. 'If I had half a brain,' he says, 'I'd be doing it properly. I'd be doing nice Stock Aitken Waterman songs, guaranteed Top Five hits. Instead S-Express stands out in the field of pop *and* the field of dance music.'

As eighties' pop stiffened under the curling tongs of stylistic device, a new, looser form of music erupted from the club scene. Traditionally an underground phenomenon relying more on individual records than star faces, the dance scene finally came overground as the boundaries between DJ, consumer and performer blurred. The experiments set up by MARRS, S-Express and later computer buffs like Adamski and Baby Ford were essentially anti-star, more active collaborations from a pool of available talent and like minds.

This way of operating has more to do with the *laissez-faire* spirit of the sixties whilst, paradoxically, bands are working with state-of-the-art technology, filtering through a wide range of international influences from Detroit techno to Algerian rai, Belgian New Beat and 'Teutonic Beat' from

Berlin. It's this open fusion that has injected an air of the unexpected into British pop.

'There's a subliminal meaning behind the whole thing,' says Baby Ford. 'In the World of Baby Ford, you start with a record, you branch out with other people to create a network. It's not a question of money or power – just a question of being able to do certain things. It might last twenty years. I'm thinking of the next generation really.'

Now the trend is for one person to be the focal point or idea, the main resource within a mini pop organisation. The notion of The Band, a separate entity of four individuals with a guitar, is in danger of becoming outdated. Pleased at not having to deal with the clash and compromise of personalities, Ford says, 'There's only one person calling the shots, and that's me. A band dilutes your ideas down. I bet for every five people in a group now there might be five people making their own records.'

Women, too, have found a voice and a style within this scene. The athletic Yazz's version of an old soul hit 'The Only Way Is Up' was the best-selling single of 1988. She and the Rochdale star Lisa Stansfield both work in collaboration with DJ Coldcut, or Jonathan More – a producer and songwriter who originally started out as a DJ in a small Deptford night-club.

Neneh Cherry is another upfront female rap singer who took on board the DIY ethics of punk to form the Cherry Bear Organisation – a conglomeration of stylists and musicians who helped to present her sweet raw image to the nation. All lycra, chains, trainers and flyaway hair, Cherry exudes a multiracial message of New-Age positivity.

'I think things are changing. After the tension of the eighties dancing has become strong again,' she says, 'Like the pre-war jitterbugs and the Lindy hop, people are letting off a lot of steam. Music has become that important again.'

Much of the appeal of the new British club music got sidetracked in the media debate about acid house. Because, shock horror, young people were taking drugs, the original purpose behind 'acid' raves and warehouse parties was ignored. Not only did young clubbers get together to get out of it, their enthusiasm became part of what's been termed Equity Culture, a loose accumulation of 'New-Age' principles. This is environmental concern with a House soundtrack, an attractive and vague humanitarianism that has meant a recovery of idealism, of lost innocence.

Dance music has been a rejuvenating and necessary force in British pop. Its very effectiveness (two-thirds of the average weekly chart in 1990 register dance hits) has posited a challenge to rock and the conventional pop format. British pop is more polarised than ever before, with guitar bands like U2 and Deacon Blue pursuing 'real' acoustic and electric instrumentation, and dance acts celebrating the tyranny of the tape loop.

Some have crossed the great divide by combining both influences – a characteristically British ability. Former independent rock bands like The Stone Roses, Happy Mondays, Primal Scream and The Beloved, schooled in the art of psychedelic feedback, are now incorporating dance styles in their music.

'It's just a love of dance music. If you enjoy something that much you can't help but want to participate,' says singer Jon Marsh of The Beloved. 'You don't set out to compete with black American dance music, you acknowledge its influence on what you do, but use it to create a kind of hybrid. Otherwise you become like The Pasadenas [A black

British R & B pop group] who are pretty good but basically a pastiche.'

The impetus for change in pop has often come through dance music. Its driving beat acts as a motor and a galvanising force. The problem now is that as the pop industry has grown, so has its financial accountability. Locked into a system of cheques and balances, record companies are loathe to take risks, drifting into the easy money of film sound-tracking and revivalist CDs.

Pop criticism has also had a part to play in quashing pop's magic. In the seventies it was still to some extent an unknown quantity, but since then it has been taken apart, restructured and decoded by performers and critics alike, till even the unexpected is expected.

In plundering the wayward imagery of the seventies, especially in his glam disco version of T. Rex's 'Children of the Revolution', Baby Ford is not only recapturing a slice of that time, but projecting it forward to his nineties viewpoint.

Likewise, The Beloved celebrate items of sixties hippie-dom with their kaftans and psychedelic riffs, but that is charged by a House beat and conspicuous references to equi-table nineties' living. 'You can't help but assimilate things you've heard over the years,' says Marsh. 'It's not till people point it out to you that you realise how directly it's affected the way you write.'

On their 1990 hit 'Hello', Marsh sings hello to a whole host of heroes and villains including: 'Little Richard, Little Nell, Willie Wonka, William Tell/Salman Rushdie and Kym Mazelle. Hello.' That arch mixing of influences from foot-ball to literature to politics and dance indicates the future for pop that may be fatigued but has no excuse to become lethargic. As Marsh says, 'Welcome to the [brave new] world . . . '

NOTES

1 Judy and Fred Vermorel, *Fandemonium!*, London, Omnibus, 1989, p. 25.

The Tied Cottage Effect

ANGELA PHILLIPS

One of the greatest attractions of tied housing is born out of the housing shortage in areas of labour shortage. Employers, quite wisely in business terms, provide housing in order to attract and retain staff. One way of abolishing much of the tied housing would be to eradicate the housing shortage.

Problems Associated with Tied Housing

Mobility: A man in a tied house can be trapped unwillingly in a job he wishes to leave, solely because he has nowhere else to live.

Exploitation: An employee in a tied house faces the risk of losing job and home simultaneously if he should 'step out of line'. The employer therefore holds all the trump cards and there are examples of this very fact leading to low wages being paid, poor quality housing not being improved, the employee having to be on call for long hours.

(From the Shelter Report on Tied Housing, Moira Constable, 1974.)

Rain again. That means wellies and raincoats, and the cover for the buggie. 'Stop wriggling, David.' It will take ten minutes longer to get ready and the bus queue will be a struggle. 'Eat your toast, darling.' Nobody wants to wait while you deal with the cover and the buggie – 'Stop teasing her' – but if I leave it off it means another set of clothes and Jodie will howl. 'Don't put your hand in your milk' – and it always takes longer in the rain. 'Oh, no, it's all over your clothes now, I will have to change them.' We'll be late again.

Rachel arrives at the works' crèche with seconds to spare and David runs off happily to find Graham. Rachel has been dreading this moment. She should have tried to explain before but couldn't bring herself to tell him. Graham won't be coming to nursery any more. David has lost so many friends. Abbie disappeared a couple of months ago to start school; Max's mother moved to another job and had to find another crèche; Graham was the one who was going to stay right until the end but his mother was sacked. No one knows why. No job – no childcare – she was told and Graham was out.

There is someone else missing too. Tahiba, his favourite nursery worker has gone. She had been at the crèche for nearly a year which is something of a record: most leave within six months for work with shorter hours and higher pay. The management has explained that childcare workers must be paid at the bottom of the scale because otherwise it would not be economic to run a nursery. The unions had been silenced by the harsh arithmetic of profit. Higher wages would mean an end to the nursery and sixty women depend on it.

So the nursery staggers on with ever-changing, badly paid, and apathetic staff. The staffing ratios are far too low.

There had been a time when the mothers could have shopped the employers to the local authority for employing seven workers to cope with nearly sixty children, but that possibility disappeared long before Rachel needed childcare, when the government decided on deregulation to encourage employers to build nurseries. They described the new arrangements as 'voluntary quality control'.

Rachel remembers the discussions dimly because she had been doing a project at school on women's employment. Some old lady had been arguing that one worker couldn't possibly work with more than three children under two. The government maintained that such high staffing ratios were a luxury. That industry needed workers and quantity must be the key word. 'After all,' the employment minister had pointed out, 'in the days before contraception, women had dealt happily with families of ten or more.' There were impassioned calls for unity in the face of an industrial crisis. She had discussed it with her friends and they all agreed that the old biddy counselling caution was a real reactionary and just trying to keep women at home. The regulations were lifted with little public dissent.

David is panicking. He's a difficult one. He has to know exactly what is happening each day and he hates to be left with strangers. Tahiba always took him away and played with him while Rachel left. This new woman is looking at him as though she has never seen a child before and doesn't know which end is up. She is almost certainly another untrained, short-term, fill-in from the dole queue.

When Rachel left, school dole queues had been a lot shorter. It was 1995 and the much discussed DTB, The Demographic Time Bomb, had finally exploded. Everyone was desperate for staff. She had got a job straight out of school with the promise of on-the-job training one week in three. Gradually she had progressed from simple filing to word-processing and office management. It was a great atmosphere to work in. Rachel really felt wanted.

It hadn't lasted. By the time David had come along the numbers of school leavers had already started to rise. She got her nursery place on the basis of long service and there were plenty desperate to take her place if she left. The baby boom of the early 1990s would soon be hitting the streets and swelling the dole queues. There were rumours that nurseries would close and employers would go back to employing only men and childless women – much as they used to do in the 1980s.

Rachel is beginning to wonder if this would be a bad thing. David is wailing and clinging to her skirt. This upsets the placid Jodie who starts to cry. Rachel looks desperately at the clock and detaches herself, choking back her own tears as she rushes towards the office. She has promised to return at lunchtime which is always a disaster. It upsets the children, upsets the staff and upsets her too.

Ms Parsons, her boss, is already in; usually that means trouble. This time she doesn't even turn away from the window. Rachel takes in the clenched fists and tight neck and retreats nervously to her desk. Ms Parsons remains there staring out of the window until the phone rings and everything becomes clear.

'Oh hallo, it's you. Yes, I did see James and do you know what the bastard told me? He has promoted that little pipsqueak, two years out of university, right over my head. It is absolutely intolerable, I simply cannot work for the man but I'm stuck. James knows I won't move the children again and he is taking advantage of it to make my life a misery.'

Ms Parson's children are in the executive school. If they

were in the ordinary nursery, she might not have been so concerned about moving them, muses Rachel. By now her boss's attention has moved to her. 'I see you have taken fifteen minutes off this morning,' she remarks sarcastically. 'You can consider it advance time off in lieu – I have an important meeting at 5.30 p.m. and I want you to stay late to take notes.'

Rachel's heart jumps, her stomach clenches, and she can feel the tears springing into her eyes. As she opens her mouth to complain Parsons cuts in: 'The reason we have a staff crèche is not to make your life easier but to improve productivity. The crèche stays open until 6.30 p.m. and there is no reason why you should not be working.' Rachel bites her tongue. She is as tied to this job as Parsons is to hers. They should be on the same side yet Parsons doesn't seem to realise that they have anything in common at all. Surely she must realise how awful it is to travel for an hour with two hungry, exhausted children.

There was a time when they would have been able to discuss the problem of childcare. Back in the heady days of the DTB, newspapers and magazines wrote about women workers as if they were all the same, with the same problems. Female executives would call meetings of women employees to discuss childcare leave and training programmes. They talked about maximising potential and assertiveness training. They allowed staff to work the hours they chose and to take extra leave in the school holidays. If employees' children were ill staff would be allowed to take a few days off, and if they needed to phone home to be reassured that the kids were all right, nobody counted the cost.

Then came the workplace nurseries. At first everyone welcomed them. It was wonderful to know that the children were well cared for and close by. The unions were out at the front urging employers to invest in childcare; women's groups were pushing them too. The employers were reluctant at first but, as staff shortages bit deeper, they realised that short-term investment in childcare could pay for itself in the long run. They started to put pressure on the government too: for tax concessions and simplified planning regulations.

Rachel remembered what it had been like in the early years. Her first boss, Ms Tremblake, had been a personnel manager at the bank with a couple of children in the crèche. She had been a staff representative on the nursery management committee and very involved in discussions about staff training and the nursery curriculum. There had been big arguments about whether to prepare children for the national curriculum or just let them enjoy themselves.

The curriculum people had won, but shortly after that staffing problems had started and it was no longer a question of educating children (by any method); the staff had their work cut out just keeping them under control. That was when Ms Tremblake started to change her tune. There were secret discussions about setting up an executive crèche. Rachel had heard a group of executives discussing the fact that they would rather leave work than allow their children's academic future to be jeopardised. The company couldn't afford to lose all those women.

The executive crèche had started as a sort of sponsored nanny-share. It was justified by the pretence that senior women needed to work longer hours and therefore needed more flexible childcare. After a while they organised a special school for 3 to 11 year-olds, to prepare the children for the public-school entrance exams. There was a special bus service which could be used by the larger branches as well as by head office. The lower-status staff members were kept out by the high fees. High fliers, helped by massive tax rebates, didn't find the cash a problem.

Once the articulate and powerful women had been creamed off into this first-class service, the secretaries and clerks felt powerless. There was always the fear that if they complained they would lose the place – no place, no job.

Rachel's mind strayed back to the nursery and David's anguished face as she left. Jodie doesn't seem to mind. She makes herself at home anywhere and her smiling face, and obliging ways, endear her even to the most inexperienced young girls. They love to dress her up like a little doll and put bows in her hair: not the most stimulating environment but at least she is happy. David, she suspects, is not. He has been getting more and more difficult. He kicks and bites her when she arrives to collect him. It's almost as though he is punishing her for leaving him. But he won't tell her anything. If she asks what he has been doing he just says: 'Nothing.'

If only she could take him out of the nursery but she cannot see how. Private childcare is far too expensive. It might be possible to find an unregistered minder but then she wouldn't be able to get any tax rebates, and anyway there was no telling what kind of care such a minder would provide. It might be even worse than the nursery. Some women manage to look after their children at home but they are the ones with husbands on high salaries. Her Greg could never have earned enough to keep them all. Anyway he left just after Jodie was born. Sometimes he pops up on a Sunday to take the children to the park but then he just melts away. He earns his living in mysterious ways, largely untraceable by the tax authorities, so his maintenance contributions are very low. She has to work to pay for the roof over their heads.

That was another thing which had changed with the great DTB. Lone parents like Rachel used to be able to stay at home and care for their children. The money they got was a pittance but they could live on it. Then came the great drive to make one-parent families self-sufficient. It had been spearheaded by one of the organisations representing one-parent families, which believed that liberating women into work would solve all their problems.

Rachel is not against earning her own living but this business of tying the job to the nursery cannot be described as freedom. Lone parents like herself are priority for the workplace nurseries but they are forced to take whatever job comes with the place. Often they end up working far below their skill level and nearly always at lower wages. They have no alternative. With the government's pro-family strategy, the one-parent family has become a social pariah. If they don't have a job they cannot live. Some councils rehouse their unemployed lone parents in hostels with communal kitchens and dormitories for the over-threes. In other areas the children are taken into care and the mothers left to fend for themselves.

Rachel considers herself lucky. She got her job and nursery place before Greg left but she dare not give it up for fear that she would be reallocated to something at a lower salary on the other side of town. The employers pat themselves on the back for providing the nursery places. In fact the lower rates paid by single mothers are subsidised by Social Services and, since the employers can give them virtually any job, usually at lower rates of pay, single mothers have become an increasingly useful source of cheap labour. There have been a few attempts to unionise them but most are in such a rush to leave work, collect their kids and get home, that they cannot attend union meetings. Anyway most of them are too afraid of victimisation.

Twelve-thirty. Rachel's heart gives a little leap of pleasure. She has given herself permission to see her children. It will be hellish, she knows, but she still cannot wait to get over there. The rain is still coming down in grey sheets. She will have to leave Jodie behind. There is no way she will struggle to get all those clothes on and off, but she has to get to the shops or they won't eat tonight. David greets her with noisy enthusiasm and makes little fuss about putting his boots and raincoat back on.

Out through the gate, his little hand in hers, the anxiety which keeps her stomach permanently clenched relaxes just for a moment. Then, quite suddenly, he slips his hand out of hers and runs down the road shouting: 'Gay-um, Gay-um.' There indeed is Graham, standing next to his mother with a tin in his hand. The children meet and dance around each other, shouting with pleasure. David joins in, happily rattling the tin with its handful of coins. Only then does Rachel see the placard leaning against the wall, already streaked from the rain. 'No Work, No Childcare, No Childcare, No Work. Please help us stay together.' The women's eyes lock for a minute and Rachel takes her struggling child away.

A CHARTER FOR WORKPLACE NURSERIES

In the current political climate the workplace nursery may seem to be the only viable option for providing the childcare that we so urgently need. Nevertheless it is an option which should be approached with caution. We tie children to profit

118

at our peril. I offer the following suggestions for the minimum safeguards necessary to protect children and workers.

1   Every workplace nursery should offer a minimum of one-third of its places to the community (to be paid for by the local authority or individual parents.) Where parents change their 'tied' jobs they should have the option of taking up one of the community places and the right to keep their own place until a community place becomes vacant.

2   Employers should not have control of the allocation of places which should be decided by a nursery committee representing parents, nursery workers, trade unions, and employers, with representation from the local community.

3   An independent inspectorate should be charged with monitoring all nurseries (private, or local authority) and ensuring that they meet legal standards in quality and safety.

4   Wherever possible children should be cared for in their own communities alongside the children who will become their school friends. To this end, trade unions should encourage employers to join with voluntary groups, and statutory bodies, to establish and support affordable, community-based childcare facilities accessible to all.

5   Campaigns for shorter working hours should be a part of a workplace policy for childcare. No nursery, however good, is a substitute for family life.

Who Cares?

JENNIFER POTTER

It was dark when I first came to Borocourt, dark and rainy.
The mansion, poorly lit, looms suddenly out of the woods,
its turrets and gargoyles tangled against the stormy sky.
'The entrance front,' notes Mark Girouard, chronicler of
Victorian country houses, ' . . . has so much piled into it
that it assumes a slightly manic quality – which makes its
present use as Borocourt Mental Hospital not inapposite.'

Inside, a few residents shuffle up and down the dismal
vaulted corridors hung with hospital direction signs and
execrable paintings on obscure historical themes. (I called
them patients, then. I didn't know.) A young man stops to
ask me for a cigarette. He stands very close, bunching his
shoulders. I hesitate. He looks almost, well, you know,
normal . . . It's bloody dark. He might just possibly be
staff. And if he isn't staff, what am I supposed to do? Could
that slightly daffy exterior conceal an arsonist at heart?
What, in God's name, are the rules? I smile too eagerly and
mumble that I no longer smoke. Failure number one, I'm
afraid.

And after the meeting is over, the meeting of the Borocourt Parents' Association, the minutes duly read and the
long-standing officers re-elected, we stay for a glass of wine

and the usual refreshments. The chaplain circulates with a plate of sausage rolls. 'May I tempt you?' is his opening line.

In the weekend I later spent at Borocourt Hospital I saw a lot of the young man who had unsuccessfully accosted me in the dark. His name is Andrew, one of 300 men and women with mental handicaps – or learning difficulties, according to the new orthodoxy – for whom Borocourt is home.

As soon as I enter the Saturday afternoon disco, Andrew waves me up on stage where he gets in everyone's way, fiddling the knobs of the very impressive equipment as he tries to work the microphone. Bushy-haired with eyes a fraction off-beam, he reminds me of an old boyfriend, two combs carried like a status symbol in the back pocket of his jeans. I wonder why he's here. The nurses counter my question by wondering why *anyone* is here; but they admit that Andrew wouldn't survive long outside. Body language, you see. He stands too close, badgering you with harmless snippets of misinformation that quickly drive you round the bend.

Andrew likes the disco. Everyone here likes the disco. It's held in the blacked-out ballroom, a lofty, wood-panelled room smelling of floor polish that retains the gaudy remnants of its Christmas decorations in late January. Father Christmas's beard glows blue in the strobe lights. The music is painfully loud: Pet Shop Boys, Tanita Tikaram, Texas's 'I Don't Want a Lover'. Down on the floor, the same contortions you see on any dancefloor, the same wall-huggers looking on. The only person who looks out of place is a neat, twinset-and-pearls sort of woman who flaps her arms like a chicken. Below my feet, among a cluster drawn by the heady beat of the amplifiers, a tiny old woman in red track suit and helmet jigs up and down; she sports a prominent black eye.

In the old days, I'm told, dances were stuffier affairs: men lined against one wall, women against the other, forbidden to dance more than twice with the same partner for fear of 'relationships'. You didn't hear much about rights, in those days, or dignity.

In Alders – the wards are named like that, Lilacs and Limes, Almonds and Poplars, Laurels and Hawthornes – the nursing philosophy is pinned to the noticeboard:

The service aims to provide an environment that promotes self-esteem, dignity and independence. To provide nursing intervention that is individualised, holistic, and emancipatory. Such intervention will be based upon the process of assessment, planning, implementation and evaluation.

I ask Eileen, one of the senior nurses, whether each ward has evolved its own philosophy. She shrugs. They've been trying to make them more realistic, she says, but the new management prefers to work towards individual goals.

It's all academic, anyway. As part of the government's policy of community care, Borocourt will close soon, the mansion transformed into time-share apartments or a country club or whatever else the planners will allow. Today's new passwords – presence in the community, choice, competency, participation and dignity – cannot open doors here, so Borocourt must go. It's hard to argue with ideals but when they were first explained to me I felt a sharp unease.

Back in the disco, Andrew nags me to say a few words into the microphone. I'm getting annoyed. Another chap thinks I've seen him before, in another hospital. He wants to know if he's grown. Above the disco din I shout something back, unaware that Andrew has just found the 'on' switch to the microphone. I'm very embarrassed, and after a decent interval I slink off stage and out through the massive wooden doors to the reception hall where seedy houseplants sprawl under a hand-written notice: 'This is not an ashtray.'

Several residents congregate by the doors, keeping the music at bay. Already I recognise some of the faces. There's Jonathan, who nestles a Coke can under his chin like a child's comforter; and Richard, the image of a prep-school master with Eamon Andrews' haircut, who promptly latches on to me as a possible ally.

'Now look here,' he says in his best buttonhole voice, 'I've lost Friday already. What if I lose all my five days next week? What then?'

I haven't a clue what he's talking about. 'I'm only a visitor,' I explain. (Later, I learn that the storms have cut off the hospital's electricity supplies and forced the temporary closure of the sheltered workshop.)

Richard won't let go. Holding up all five fingers of one hand he repeats slowly and carefully. 'My five days. What if I lose them all next week? What will you do then?' Lost to his solipsism, Richard came here when his mother died, an event that failed to register though they lived together in the same house.

I am saved by a man in a black helmet who asks if I know Natland. I do, surprisingly. It's a hamlet in Cumbria. 'Does it have any shops yet?' he asks in a nasal whine. While I wonder whether to tell him about the Asda supermarket under construction just a mile down the road, he launches

123

into a complicated anecdote about his father and taking some bellows on the Underground. The story tails off and we're back to shops in Natland. I marvel at the patience of other people.

Community care means providing the services and support which people who are affected by problems of ageing, mental illness, mental handicap or physical or sensory disability need to be able to live as independently as possible in their homes, or in 'homely' settings in the community. The Government is firmly committed to a policy of community care which enables such people to achieve their full potential.

(Caring for People: Community Care in the Next Decade and Beyond, Cm 849, London, HMSO, November 1989.)

Outside, it's pitch dark and the storm is blowing up again. I think I see a figure struggling with a walking-frame near the rhododendrons but my glasses are wet and I'm feeling snappy right now. A huge sign, blue and white like a motorway's, warns drivers to watch out for patients. To many, this sign is an insult but nonetheless an improvement on one from my childhood. Cripples Crossing, it said; I thought it was the name of the road.

Along the drive at intervals are clusters of villa blocks, the wards, built in the 1940s and 1960s, mostly red-brick council in style but you can't see much in the dark which intensifies the feeling of a world apart, a cross between a down-at-heel boarding school and a German prison camp. Tonight I shall take the hospital minibus to the Nurses' Home and look forward to getting out.

Jane, the senior nurse for Saturday, is taking me to a party for the 'kids' of Hazels – eight profoundly disturbed young men and women, now in their twenties, who grew up together at Borocourt, moved *en groupe* to Smith Hospital, returned when Smith closed down. A few have got away, like Margaret who now lives in a community hostel with her equally disturbed sister and one other resident. At the party, Margaret is sandwiched by two of her carers. One of them, Victoria, tells me she had renounced a previous career in catering expressly to confront her own fear of mental handicap. After twelve months in the hostel, she feels at ease with her three charges but coming to Borocourt has resurrected the old ghosts. As we talk, Margaret rocks herself back and forwards and does not speak.

The party spread is magnificent: sausage rolls, mince pies, crisps, pizza, sandwiches, a plate of smoked mackerel, punch and wine and a cup of tea for me. Someone calls me a party pooper behind my back. There are children running wild and loud party music. One of the 'kids' falls off his chair and must be helped upright again. Parents have come, and friends, but no one from outside which was the whole point of the party: to bring in volunteers.

Jane takes me to a ward upstairs where I find again the strange young woman clutching a teddy bear. Her name is June. On a previous visit she had crept up behind me in the sheltered workshop and nuzzled at the back of my hair. This time she licks my handbag and asks repeatedly to go to the party. They won't let her at first, because she grabs and causes a fuss, but they relent eventually and June is as good as gold. The trouble is caused by someone else, a beautiful girl who clacks her teeth and throws the plate of mackerel fillets in the air.

Sharon, the nurse in charge, comes from Yorkshire. June is her favourite, if favourites are allowed. We talk in the nurses' cubicle, smoking and drinking tea. It's years since I've been among people who smoke as much as here. The wallpaper flaps off the wall like flags. Outside the door a woman watches us, burping catastrophically.

I ask Sharon why she chose to work in mental handicap; a question I asked of everyone. She had tried general nursing, she says, but couldn't take it: the patients moaned all the time and she was perhaps (Yorkshire laugh) brusque with them. Here they don't answer back, which isn't meant to imply that she's unkind.

We're all tired. Jane, the senior nurse, rests her head on June's shoulder and strokes her hand.

The ward is undergoing redecoration, so the women must sit, eat, live and watch television in the same small room. They don't like each other much and friction often erupts. 'They wind you up,' I'm told, 'like families.' One misshapen body rolls across a chair in the corner. The dormitories are bare – June is not the only one to steal – except for a few soft toys lying on the candlewick bedspreads.

It's my last visit of the day. I'm talking to Jim, the Irish nurse in charge of Limes. Despite his thirty-five years at Borocourt, Jim looks the reincarnation of his previous RAF self: white shirt, tie, brylcreemed hair. His wife works here too, one of the last to retain her nurse's uniform. Beyond our observation room, the ward lies in virtual darkness.

A resident barges in and out, shaking me by the hand, 'Chenny, isn't it?' he says each time.

On about the fourth repeat, he fingers my watch. 'That's gold,' he declares, as if in accusation.

Jim starts to look apprehensive.

'Not very good gold,' I reply.

'But gold?'

'Y . . . es.'

The man staggers off.

Jim relaxes and explains that the previous night the man had started a similar conversation with one of the nurses who wore a gold brooch at her throat. 'That's gold, isn't it?' he had said and punched her in the face.

The next time the man reappears, I wish Jim hadn't told me that.

Victoria was right to talk of her fear of mental handicap. These people touch a raw nerve – *there but for the grace of God* – and so we have shut them away, out of sight, in Gothic piles like Borocourt, for being wild and rebellious, for stealing washing off someone else's line, for kicking the horses, for having an illegitimate child, for being ugly and stupid, for being 'not quite right'.

Today's solution is just as savage: to sprinkle them back into a distinctly uncaring community, stirring the pot until the problem disappears, and all in the name of greater humanity.

That, at least, is how I felt before I came to Borocourt. Now, I'm not so sure. The ground has shifted so many times that my certainties aren't certainties any more.

You see, I am not unengaged. I have a friend whose son lives at Borocourt – has lived here since he was 12. He is now 33. When I think of the future – all those fine phrases about participation and dignity – I wonder what will happen to Peter.

Diagnosed as autistic, Peter cannot speak, though he grunts expressively and twists his long white fingers into a rudimentary sign language I cannot understand. His grandmother maintains he would have made a fine concert pianist – his little 'difficulties' apart – choosing to remain ambitious in her might-have-beens. Peter has, in any case, an obviously sweet nature and likes to be kissed – on both cheeks – when you visit.

My friend comes as often as he can. The rituals are well-established. First, as they drive away from Borocourt, my friend squirts soapy water on to the windscreen. Peter laughs. After several more jokes – like blowing raspberries on their forearms – they stop briefly in Henley-on-Thames for sandwiches and ice-cream, then drive into the countryside looking for somewhere to park. Peter is by now quite agitated.

When I was with them, we stopped eventually in the woods, our way blocked by fallen trees as the storm had passed only a few days before. It was as good a place as any. Peter leant forward from the back seat and for nearly ten minutes, while I looked the other way, my friend gently and lovingly massaged the head of his grown-up son.

Who will do this to Peter when his father isn't around any more and Peter is left on his own? Would you do it? Would I? Because however right and righteous are the *principles* of community care – and the government's White Paper, *Caring for People*, pushes all the right bootstrap buttons of choice and independence and achieving one's full potential – it's the practice I'm worried about.

Do not, in any case, be misled into thinking that the brave new forms of service envisaged by *Caring for People* have yet taken shape, at least on a scale sufficient to accommodate those people who now live in our institutions or those who might have come here, at other times. And whatever the government's declared vision, one may wonder if it is not a little cavalier to play pass the parcel with people's lives.

When Borocourt closes down, some time within the next decade, its residents will lose the added extras of institutional life: the gymnasium with its exercise bicycle, climbing ropes and adult trampoline; the weekend discos; the swimming pool; the playing fields complete with vandalised changing hut; the sheltered workshop and Sessions Room, housed in what looks like a large, L-shaped Nissen hut, together with the Music Room – a cheery place decorated with dolls and posters of the stars: Michael Jackson, Eddy Grant, Richard Clayderman – where an ageing, good-hearted music teacher, who came to Borocourt from panto, plays the piano with a wiggle and aplomb.

In return, the residents will gain the privilege of living with – and like – the rest of us. I suspect that's what frightens me most. Shut the place down by all means, give the poor sods a chance to breathe and live a decent, ordinary life. But not in my street. Not in my community. I mean, what would happen to the children; and the traffic? No, it wouldn't do here.

The Government acknowledges that the great bulk of community care is provided by friends, family and neighbours. The decision to take on a caring role is never an easy one. However, many people make that choice and it is right that they should be able to play their part in looking after those close to them. But it must be recognised that carers need help and support if they are to continue to carry out their role; and many people will not have carers readily available who can meet all their needs.

(*Caring for People: Community Care in the Next Decade and Beyond*, Cm 849, London, HMSO, November 1989.)

My second full day at Borocourt. I'm up early, having spent

the night at Caversham Hill Nurses Home (charge: £2.45, receipt duly acknowledged by post) and caught the staff minibus back to the hospital. After a fried breakfast in the staff canteen, I wander round the grounds on my own. The light is a deep, soft yellow, picking out each detail of the mansion's Venetian façade with its heraldic beasts and sharp crocketed gables.

Built around 1876 for Edward Hermon, cotton magnate and MP for Preston, the house with its 246-acre estate was sold in 1932 to the local authorities of Buckinghamshire, Oxfordshire, Reading and Oxford, by Hermon's son-in-law, Robert Trotter Hermon-Hodge, first Baron Wyfold of Accrington. The 'Boro' of Borocourt is an acronym: wishing to distance itself from the 'taint' of mental handicap, the family refused to allow the continued use of its original name, Wyfold Court.

At a more respectable hour, I join Eileen on Alders. As the senior nurse on duty, she's busy telephoning all seventeen wards to remind them that power and water must be rationed as the emergency generators are still in use. This means no baths, upsetting residents and staff who live at Esther Carling House which lost its power when the lines to Borocourt went down: without electricity, the house has no lights, no heat, no hot water, no cooking facilities; no generator, either. With most of the estate families eating at the canteen, food supplies are running low: it feels like we're living under siege.

As Eileen makes her telephone calls, Howard, one of Borocourt's few black residents, comes in for a cigarette; they're kept in the staff drawer. He is sent away to button up his trousers. After several abortive attempts, he succeeds by changing into a pair of jeans, fastened at the top but chopped off at mid-calf; he looks like a castaway.

130

I'm running low myself. At 10 a.m. I go over to the mansion for the Sunday service but the chaplain never shows and after drifting in to the video show I help the Irish porter put away the chairs in the ballroom. He lives at Esther Carling, devoting his money and all his spare time to the opera.

Then back to Eileen and a tour of the wards. Already gaining in confidence, I fall into the easy trap of developing theories with my newly-acquired impressions; the theory, for example, that you can judge the capabilities of each group of residents by the smell of their quarters, a scale that ranges from the musty tang of urine at one end to hospital polish at the other. Like government policy, however, this theory is soon confounded by its opposite: that the swankier, spick-and-span wards have robbed the inmates of their right to live as they please.

But the details remain, even if I cannot string them together into a 'case': a row of wash-basins from which the tap-heads have been removed; Muffin the Mule paraded as decoration in a ward for old people; the designer jodhpurs of a nurse in the Regional Secure Unit, her keys carried on a long leather thong; a small, sandy-haired young man turned to the wall, his arms encased in plastic splints to forestall his self-destruction; the palpable affection of a young care assistant towards his charges, whose wreck is physical as well as mental.

To my outsider's eyes, the staff appear patient, caring and kind (there must be exceptions, but I never noticed any); they keep going in spite of their own uncertain future, for when Borocourt closes down, they must disperse too, into the community.

At length I encounter one who expresses less optimism than the others. One of his residents is leaving soon and he fears she may be very lonely. Sometimes, he says, he watches them returning to work at the factory after lunch, twitching, sniffing their fingers, grinning at the sky. They look like aliens, he says. People from Mars. How would they fit in, out there?

The Government recognises that some people will continue to need residential or nursing-home care. For such people, this form of care should be a positive choice. And there will be others, in particular elderly and seriously mentally ill people and some people with serious mental handicap, together with other illnesses or disabilities, whose combination of health and social care needs is best met by care in a hospital setting.

(Caring for People: Community Care in the Next Decade and Beyond, CM 849, London, HMSO, November 1989.)

At the very end of my visit, I go to see Peter in Lilacs. It needed a certain courage. I had been here before with his father but now I am on my own.

From the outside, Lilacs looks much like all the other wards: a red-brick, single-storey villa set among trees.

Inside is different. Lilacs, you see, is the pits, the place for no-hopers, the sort described as 'challenging', where nineteen men are cared for by three, at most four staff on duty with just enough time to see that the men are fed and watered and little time to spare.

When I sought permission to come to Borocourt, Lilacs was one of the wards they wanted me to see. Lilacs is part of their argument, not as a showpiece but because it represents all that is bad about institutional care. There must, they say, be something better than this, something that will give the men a chance.

Peter's father can't see this. Profoundly grateful for the care his son receives, he's terrified that soon they will close Lilacs down and shunt its residents out into the community. His fears are shared by the Borocourt Parents' Association. 'The profoundly handicapped or disturbed cannot lead normal lives in the community,' they say. 'Sadly, they cannot lead "normal" lives anywhere.' Some of the parents have cared for their children at home for many years and know what they're talking about. For them, Borocourt represents the final safety net and now that the net is to be snatched away, who will 'care' for their children when they're gone? What will happen when the government finally gets its sums right and discovers that good community care costs a damn sight more than what we're spending already?

I found Peter in the bleak barn of a day-room, sitting with the others on scuffed, uncomfortable chairs. Some of the men stare at the lino tiles; others have cranked up their heads to watch a television suspended near the ceiling. A few pictures adorn the walls – too high to contemplate – and an empty, wrought-iron plant holder.

Appearing to recognise me, Peter comes over to be kissed then returns to his seat and staring at the floor.

'We do our best within the limitations of our environment,' says Henry, the black nurse who stands stiffly and looks to the right of your eyes. I like Henry and his evident unease. He wants to be proud but he wants equally to be honest.

In the centre of the room, a man lies face down on the floor.

'Underfloor heating,' explains Henry. 'He likes to keep warm.'

The last time they tried to improve Lilacs the man who now lies on the floor provoked a riot and the place was wrecked. After the debris was swept away, life returned to normal. They don't like change, on Lilacs.

Outside in the corridor, other men pass and re-pass in front of the office. One looks smart – he's spent the afternoon with his family – and smiles. The others resemble tramps, stained and spotted with their flies undone. They don't smell, however; the staff keep them clean.

James, wearing a grubby brown mac, sidles up to me and glares into my eyes. Yesterday, when we'd come to take Peter to the woods, James's mood had been ebullient. 'I like tea,' he had said, 'tea and biscuits. On those Winceyette tables.' The mock-rustic tables and chairs are bolted to the floor in the style of a particularly nasty motorway café. 'Is it tea-time yet? I like tea. Tea and biscuits.' Today his eyes look lost and he has a crusted cut on his chin. It's left to me to talk about tea; tea and biscuits.

Peter used to have a friend on Lilacs, one of the ugliest men you ever saw with a pitted pulpy face and a nose the size of a potato. Like my father-in-law, a retired colonel, his greatest ambition was to be a traffic warden. At last he inveigled his family into giving him a traffic-warden's uniform, God knows how.

Out on the ward's small parking lot, he ran a tight ship. 'What d'you think you're doing, sunshine?' he used to bellow at my friend.

One day, during the long, hot summer he appeared in boots and traffic-warden's hat but quite naked in between. My friend, who had parked by the front door, smiled tentatively through the open window. The other foamed with rage. 'Just because I'm not wearing the full gear,' he bellowed, 'doesn't mean I can't throw the book at you.'

I saw no traffic warden, on my visit, and Peter had no obvious friend.

The men sleep in three dormitories: seven beds in the centre room, six beds in the rooms on either side, each with its cheap, veneered wardrobes, shiny floors and lack of ornament. The men would smash things, I'm told, or steal.

'And maybe,' says the nurse, 'they don't need their knick-knacks around them as much as women do.'

I remember Muffin the Mule. It belonged to the sister, not to the women. 'They don't dare touch Muffin,' she had said. 'They'd have me to deal with if he came to any harm.'

The man who has been lying on the floor shoots through the door and scuttles under one of the beds. We make no move to entice him from his hiding place.

Question: is it better to respect an individual's right to do whatever he or she pleases, even if the chosen action is demeaning; or should one encourage the sort of behaviour likely to gain respect?

'We shouldn't talk in front of the residents as if they're not here,' says Eileen and we leave.

Andrew was the last person I saw at Borocourt, the first and the last. I was standing outside the mansion house, in the dark, waiting for the 6 p.m. minibus to take me to the station. Although it was a wet, blustery night, Andrew had removed his jacket and hunched his shoulders into mine. Whenever I moved, he moved too so there wasn't much point.

'The bus doesn't run on Sundays,' he volunteered.

'It does,' I said, 'I've checked.'

'Not on Sundays.'

That night, I was its only passenger. The storm was blowing up again and I wanted to get home. I wanted a drink, too. My attempts at conversation with the woman bus driver fell flat and I was glad to get to Reading and the train. Back in London, on the tubes, the prickly odour of incontinence clung to my clothes like a bad dream. The tube was crowded, young people, mainly, going out for the night, and as I looked at their city-sleek faces, so sure of themselves and of their world, I wondered who it was who came from Mars.

With special thanks to Bob Rhodes, Eileen Tollafield and Jane Ireland. To protect their identities, the names of the residents have been changed.

Homelessness

SHEILA McKECHNIE

If you were planning a housing programme, the first thing you would do is assess need. Yet that is what the government has singularly failed to do since the publication of the 1977 Green Paper. There is no absolute definition of need but that in itself is no argument against an attempt to quantify the problem. The National Housing Forum[1] has recently published such an estimate, resolving in the process some of the problems of definitions. By their estimates we are currently between 1,200,000 and 2,000,000 homes short in England and Wales, and if we carry on as we are this will rise to 3–4,000,000 by the turn of the century.

There are underlying social changes in society that mean our housing stock needs to expand: the growth of single person households; the fact that we are all living longer; the trends in relationship breakdown, etc. However, none of these factors would have resulted in our current crisis if there had not been major cuts in housing investment, particularly in low cost housing for rent for those unable to buy.

It is the size of the cuts in housing investment that is the major factor in the current crisis. By 1982–3 cuts in housing accounted for more than 75% of all government cuts in

137

public expenditure.[2] In 1978–9 housing made up 6.8% of all public spending. By 1989–90 it had been cut back to 1.6%.[3] By 1987 the proportion of GDP being spent on housing in the UK had fallen to 3.7%.[4] This puts the UK at the bottom of the league table of most European countries in terms of housing investment. Yet these figures fail to reveal the extent of the problem for those groups in society unable to buy. In the mid-seventies local authorities and housing associations together were producing about 230,000 units of affordable housing a year in Britain. By 1991 council building will virtually have ceased and the much trumpeted housing association programme will be producing about 35,000 units a year. Even this latter figure is greeted with scepticism in the housing-association movement. Much new housing association stock will be at higher rent levels than homeless families can afford and the distribution of resources means that little impact will be made in areas of greatest homelessness.

Central and local government have been playing cat and mouse games with housing since the mid-seventies. Central government determined to end the role of local authorities in housing provision and local authorities devised more and more bizarre deals to try to protect their programme. With the implementation of the Local Government and Housing Act 1989 these games will effectively cease as the Department of the Environment has under this legislation a firm hold on both new-build programmes and rent levels. Even the limited use of capital receipts for housing will in future have to be used to clear housing debts. If capital receipts from sales are excluded expenditure in housing is at record low levels in real terms in recent history.

The cut in supply of local-authority and housing-association homes would not have created the current crisis if there had been an alternative source or sources of housing. Owner-occupation has grown, aided significantly by the right to buy, but has not met the needs of low income groups.

INCREASE IN OWNER OCCUPATION

Stock of Dwellings by Tenure
England

	Rented from local authorities and New Towns		Owner-Occupation		Rented from Private Owners Housing Associations and other Tenures		Total
	000	%	000	%	000	%	000
1966	3,932	26.7	7,197	48.4	3,756	25.2	14,885
1975	4,872	28.7	9,385	55.3	2,707	16.0	16,964
1980	5,171	28.8	10,451	58.2	2,341	13.0	17,963
1985	4,627	24.8	11,836	63.5	2,185	11.8	18,648
1989	4,170	21.6	13,163	68.1	2,000	10.3	19,332

There are also strong signals that owner-occupation has reached the limits of expansion. Recent work by Glen Bramley at SAUS[5] shows that less than 10% of new households in London can afford to buy a three bedroom house at current price levels. Both high capital costs and high interest rates have combined to make owner-occupation a very insecure form of housing with significant rises in mortgage default.

Building Society repossession, United Kingdom

		Mortgages 6–12 months in arrears
1979	2,530	8,420
1980	3,020	13,490
1981	4,240	18,720
1982	5,950	23,790
1983	7,320	25,580
1984	10,870	41,940
1985	16,770	49,620
1986	20,930	45,250
1987	22,930	48,220
1988	16,090	37,200
1989	13,780	58,380

(Council of Mortgage Lenders)

The only other form of housing, private renting, has if anything fared worse. The current dogma that public is bad and private is good has less resonance in housing than in any other field.

Throughout this country private renting has been the tenure of last resort, providing the worst standards at highest cost. Over 1,000,000 rented homes have been lost from the private sector since 1976. Rent deregulation and the reduction of security of tenure have not reversed the pattern of decline although they may have stabilised the market at its more expensive end. This does not have a significant impact on poorer households except at the bed and breakfast end of the market, where private landlords are in fact subsidised by local authorities desperate to meet their legal duties to homeless households, but obliged to pay nearly twice as much (in London) for this doubtful privilege than for new local authority homes.

Private renting has provided the main source of housing for young people leaving home including students. However, rising rents are pricing many young people out of this market. Land and building costs place considerable restrictions on the expansion of the private rented market.

Aggregate figures, therefore, underestimate the shortfall of housing for lower income households. The great fallacy in the current approach is that 'the market will provide'. No single market in housing exists. Land and building costs dictate a level below which supply will simply dry up. What then for those who simply cannot afford what is on offer? The answer is all too visible on our streets.

In recent decades Britain's housing system has had two main components. Social housing has been provided to meet need while access to owner-occupation and private renting has been based on ability to pay.

Need was defined by the Housing (Homeless Person's) Act 1977 (now incorporated in the 1985 Housing Act, Part III) and is essentially restricted to certain priority groups: households with children, a pregnant woman, or someone who is vulnerable on account of their age, disability or illness. Very few single people have a right to local authority housing.

As the number of local authority houses and flats available to rent declines through a combination of the right to buy, the decline in new build and the deterioration of the stock, some local authorities in the high pressure areas simply do not have enough housing to meet their legal obligations. They are simply stacking up homeless households in various forms of temporary accommodation. Housing associations have historically made little contribution to housing homeless families and while this may increase in the next few years it will not meet the current shortfall. It will also have the negative effect of cutting the supply to single people where in the past the housing associations have made a small but significant contribution.

The decline in supply of housing to meet need has also been matched by a decline in quality. Homeless households get what is available, not what they want. What is available is often the local authority 'mistakes' of the sixties and seventies. The concentration of poorer households in run down, badly designed and badly managed estates has grown now into a major social nightmare, the consequences of which are well documented in many inner-city areas.

In a market, what decides access to housing is ability to pay. For many disadvantaged groups this is crucially determined by levels of state support through housing benefit. Ignoring owner-occupation, which is generally unavailable to those on benefit, housing costs and housing subsidies have been moving in opposite directions. As rents have risen fewer people have rights to housing benefit. There have been nine cuts in housing benefit since 1981.

Sixteen- and seventeen-year-olds not on Youth Training Schemes have been hit hardest of all. In September 1988 the government withdrew income support from the vast majority of under 18-year-olds, who get no benefit at all if they are not on a YTS scheme. Under 25-year-olds now get lower rates of Income Support and Housing Benefit payments. Payments are made in arrears, and grants to cover deposits, key money and essential furniture needed to move into a home are not available under the Social Fund. These and other changes make it extraordinarily difficult for young people to afford anywhere to live. The new destitute young begging on our streets are a direct result of these cuts.

With the general shortfall in supply and the rising costs of housing it may seem unnecessary to ask who loses and who gains as the answer is so obvious. Any group with resources below the level that gives them the choice of owner-occupation or renting loses out; the young, the black and ethnic population, single parents, disabled people, indeed everyone who loses out in a range of other fields such as employment, education and health.

Yet the question of who loses and who gains is fundamental to the political arithmetic of housing. For those who had either become owner-occupiers or who were in good quality local authority housing by the mid-seventies, the housing lottery has been equivalent to winning the football pools. Rising capital values have produced massive shifts in private wealth.

Even those struggling to get into the system, often buying on two, three or even four joint incomes, have been relatively uncritical as they too saw the long-term gains. Prolonged high interest rates and declining capital values may take the shine off the advantages of owner-occupation but the underlying tax and social advantages remain considerable.

The losers have been the majority of the under-35s and those disadvantaged by unemployment, racism, sickness, disability or just general poverty. Women predominate in all the categories of social disadvantage.

If those who lost in the housing lottery were predominantly those marginalised by our society in general, then the only hope for change would be that their housing situation had become a moral and political outrage, unacceptable in a civilised society. This is indeed the view taken by some, but in recent years its weight has rarely counterbalanced the rampant individualism and growing selfishness in our society. But there is more weight being added to the scales by those for whom the current housing system does not work, and many of these are not groups normally associated with the political marginals.

If only 10% of new households in the South East are owner-occupied that leaves an awful lot of new households in housing difficulty. The consequences of an ageing, relatively privileged, group of owner-occupiers who have a stake in the status quo are rapidly being offset by the needs of employers for labour in high-cost areas, and the declining quality of life in our cities where the cost of services are pushed higher by wage costs which in turn are pushed higher by housing and related costs. The adverse consequences of the current system on all aspects of our lives are rapidly outweighing the advantages.

However the gains from owner-occupation will not be given up lightly and the major engine of change in housing may not be either altruistic or indeed within the housing world itself. Change when it comes is much more likely to come from the impact of housing on the wider economy. This is only recently becoming the subject of popular discussion with a few notable exceptions.

Early in the 1980s Martin Pawley first raised the issue of housing and consumption. He labelled this 'reverse monopoly': have house make money! Until recently few economic models have incorporated housing equity as a factor in consumer demand. Yet in the real world everyone knows someone whose standard of living has improved directly as a result of buying in the right place at the right time. No other productive effort in work, investment in industry or savings could have produced a similar result for the majority of gainers. Yet the economy as a whole has lost. Industrial investment has declined and consumer spending is adding to a perilous balance of payments' crisis. The housing system not only has become unstable itself but has had a major impact on the economy as a whole.

Significant numbers of people in no need themselves are about to inherit considerable sums in property wealth from their parents and grandparents. Some have even ensured this eventuality by encouraging elderly relatives with good council tenancies to buy their homes for no other reason than to make money. The distributive effects of this on extremes of wealth and poverty have not been quantified, but the adverse effects on the economy as a whole are beginning to raise the shout: there must be another way.

And indeed there is but that is another whole debate. It may seem odd for the Director of Shelter to have written an article about housing which is so devoid of the moral and social arguments. There are such arguments and they are widely shared beyond organisations like Shelter. But change when it comes will be driven more by economic necessity than moral virtue. In one sense this is good. Any change in housing strategy based on the need for housing for the poor will inevitably be poor housing. If the lessons of the past have anything to teach it is that the majority as a whole has to benefit or see the potential benefit of collective social responsibility. If individualism produces the goods then individualism will triumph. Individualism in housing is not producing the goods for growing numbers. It is time now to ask what kind of housing system do we really want or rather what kind of housing system will meet *my* needs. Do not bother asking what kind of system meets the needs of the homeless. It is the wrong question, it produces the wrong answers. Everybody wants from housing what you want. Do not patronise the homeless by assuming that they are different.

NOTES

[1] *Housing Needs in the 1990s: An Interim Assessment*, National Housing Forum, 1989.

[2] Quoted in *The Evaluation of Local Authorities' Housing Spending in the 1980s*, Roberts and Kleinman, Cambridge, University of Cambridge, 1984, p. 7.

[3] From Government Public Expenditure Plans.

[4] Quoted in *Homelessness in Britain*, John Greve with Elizabeth Currie, Joseph Rowntree Memorial Trust, 1990, p. 2.

[5] *Bridging the Affordability Gap*, Glen Bramley, School of Advanced Urban Studies, University of Bristol, February 1990.

Growing Old – Not what it used to be

VIRGINIA IRONSIDE

Those of us who are now middle-aged are the first generation that declared in the sixties that we would never get
old. The Who wanted to die before they got old, The Beatles
had a mawkish view of old age that never rang true in
'When I'm Sixty-four', and indeed I caught myself recently
wittering on in an equally mawkish way to a friend along
the lines of: 'We'll probably still be raving about Elvis when
we're both sitting knitting in our rocking chairs.' Hearing
myself, I pulled myself up with a shock. What an utterly
ridiculous thing to say. Not about Elvis, of course, but the
bit about the knitting and the rocking chair. Because there's
no way I'm ever going to be knitting in a rocking chair
when I'm old. The phrase was a jokey euphemism for an
old age that none of our generation can properly anticipate.
My grandmother *did* knit and she did have a rocking chair
– she even had white hair tied into a bun; my grandfather
walked about in a tweed suit and planted young trees and
rubbed apples with his hands and banged at things with a
stick like old men should. But the old age that they lived is

an old age of the past, not the present. As Paul Valery said: 'The future is not what it used to be.'

It's not that the sixties' generation don't really *believe* they'll get old. They do. But they don't see getting old as becoming gradually more and more decrepit. It's more a case of their feeling perpetually young, but as time goes by becoming aware that there are simply more hazards – flying missiles such as cancer, Alzheimer's disease, arthritis, Parkinson's disease – that they've got to duck and weave to avoid.

There's even a new word with radical overtones, 'ageism', that's creeping into the language. In his refreshingly right-on book, *A Good Age*, Dr Alex Comfort points out that there's little difference between the old and the young except that the old have lived longer. 'Don't put up with being addressed by nurses, aides and others as "Granny", "Dad" or the like,' he advises tartly. 'Point out acidly that you have a name and if they don't know it they can damn well ask and that you were earning a living when they were still eating babyfood.'

The advertisement for a pension plan which features a man slowly getting older and older and more and more worried, highlights our confusion about what age means to this generation. The artist, no doubt this side of 40 himself, has no problem with the young man; and he shows the same man as middle-aged by receding his hair; but he's completely defeated by the old man. All he can do is cover the young man's face with lines as if he's been clawed with a rake. It could be that the illustrator's a lousy artist, or that he can't bring himself to draw the man as old, but it's more likely that his problems arise because he really can't quite anticipate how a young man today will look when he's old. And he's right to tread warily. A man with a face like a walnut and a white beard just doesn't ring true for this generation of future oldies. Even today's grannies wear jeans.

It's the same with photos of middle-aged people used to illustrate middle-aged topics. If you bought any book on the menopause even five years ago, the cover would probably have shown a woman in a white cardigan and pleated sensible skirt, with greying hair in a 'soft' set, middle-aged spread and lots of wrinkles, looking out at a heather-clad scene and accompanied by a husband who would invariably have been sitting in a car, his age only given away by his full head of greying hair and his driving gloves. This cover clearly told us that at the age of her menopause the wife and her husband had both retired (though she looked as if she'd never worked), and that their lives were now devoted to 'taking things easy', a phrase that rather sticks in the throats of the present-day middle-aged.

Buy a book on the menopause today and you'll find a different but equally confusing story. The photograph on this cover is of a creepily young-looking woman who has either been taking HRT by the sackful or has had a million-pound face-lift; in her Dallas-like coiffure there isn't a grey hair in sight and we know she's still employed in a stimulating career because she's wearing one of those ghastly Mrs Thatcher-type cravats tied into a bow, sprouting over an executive suit.

Look at one of the current crop of magazines for older people (the expression 'the elderly' is out) and you might well mistake it for *Just Seventeen*. Either the cover girl (woman?) is under 30 or the lens of the camera had been covered with so much vaseline it must have needed six strong men to steady the tripod.

And the general confusion that surrounds getting older

these days isn't helped by one's teenage children – to whom, a generation ago, one might have looked to for a lead. I've always fancied the idea of becoming a furious, crusty old parent who during my son's teenage years would be forever shouting: 'Turn the damn thing down!' or 'You can't go out in *that!*', or bemoaning the fact that he wasn't listening to the lovely songs of yesteryear that I listened to in my youth. It would be a sign of my maturity. It would fit nicely into a proper scheme of things. I say 'proper' but of course I should say 'old' scheme of things – because today it's not like that.

Today I get a son who is, to all intents and purposes, exactly as I was at that age. I honestly thought the last time I would throw a heap of clothes into the washing machine with five tubs of black Dylon was 1963 – but here I am again, on the same old bandwagon, sifting through his clothes, scraping my fingers with pumice-stone and wondering what else could go into the machine to give him the ultra-cool look he desires. (That's right – cool. Back in again.)

I had hoped at least for some interesting new music from him – but no. He even bought a tape of The Kinks the other day and raves about The Stones and Jimi Hendrix. Far from telling him to turn his music down, I find myself rummaging around my old albums to search out little-known tracks he hasn't heard of (but he usually has) or borrowing his tapes to remind myself of numbers I'd forgotten.

My son's room is plastered with pictures of Marilyn Monroe and Elvis Presley – just like mine used to be – and is painted a fashionable dark grey. In my day it was brown, but the general gloomy ambiance is just the same. By his bed lies a copy of *On the Road* by Jack Kerouac.

Something's gone wrong with the time system. Everything's got muddled up. And it'll get worse, because since most of us had children later than our own parents, and since our children will probably live with us for longer (they can't afford to move out), there's much more chance of them keeping us younger even longer.

The nearest I've got to feeling pushed into the front line in a kind of 'shove along a space, Mum, I'm moving up' is when we go to the theatre and my son will insist, under the guise of a kind of charming gallantry, on taking the tickets, guiding me across roads by gripping my arm, taking my purse as I look for the change for a programme and organising it himself, and sighing, after the show, as I try my car key in a similar blue Metro to my own. Try as I might to assure him I've *never* been able to distinguish one car from another, I know what he thinks: he thinks I'm past it. The exasperated cry of 'Oh, Mum!' has turned into the kinder: 'Let *me* do it, Mum.' But that's about it. The younger generation may be trying to nudge the older into the metaphorical rocking chair quicker than we want to go, but they're not pushing very hard. Far from bursting on to the scene with a threatening roar as we did in the sixties, they seem a rather mild and childish Kylie Minogueish bunch. Nothing to worry about.

As one gets older, too, what seems 'old' changes. I recently re-read in my diary, written when I was 18, that I was going out with someone who was OK except for one big drawback – his age. '*Incredibly* old – thirty!!!' When I was 25, 40 seemed incredibly old, and at 35, 50 seemed incredibly old. At 46 I've learned to keep my big mouth shut about what I consider to be old age because I know the goalposts keep shifting. All I'm prepared to say is that 60 seems to me to be on the spring-chickenish side.

Today I imagine that it'll be nice to be 50 because I've never enjoyed being 'late' anything. (At 29 one's in one's late twenties; at 34 one's still in one's early thirties. Wouldn't it be better to be in one's early nineties than one's late fifties?) But who knows how I'll feel when I'm older.

Because all one's views about the future change with the passing of time. At 15 if you've not got a steady boyfriend or girlfriend you may feel on the shelf and have to be reminded there's plenty of time ahead; at 40 you don't need reminding there's *not* plenty of time ahead. (The fact that life is finite and death is a reality is an idea that only popped into my head about five years ago and it won't pop out again.) The theory is that time goes quicker as we get older because as each year passes it's a smaller fraction of our past life. For instance, on reaching 2 years old the toddler will feel that ages have passed since he was 1 – and they have. One half of his life, in fact. On his 50th birthday, a man may feel the previous year since he was 49 has simply flashed by – and it has. One fiftieth of his whole life. A mere nothing.

How one views one's own age changes, too. At 15 one wanted nothing more than to be thought older, in middle age one wants nothing more than to be thought younger, while most oldies I know seem to take a pride in their great age, announcing shamelessly: 'I'm 90 you know!' Will we be like that? Or will 90 seem a mere nothing? Will we all live longer? Will we have found cures for the ills of old age? If so, then what? It's all a mystery.

In middle age one at least has the maturity to know that one doesn't know. Ever since I realised that I adored Jane Austen when I was 15, gobbled her up again at 25 and that today I could take her or leave her and preferably leave her, I've not trusted my judgement. Which is my 'real' opinion?

Was liking Jane Austen 'just a phase?' Or is not liking Jane Austen 'just a phase?'

Defy old age as one will, it is definitely there, lurking around. And it's those odd flashes of tell-tale behaviour which say more than a million brown spots on the backs of the hands, white hairs, wrinkles, receding gums, reading glasses and stringy necks.

For instance: in the last year I've ordered a sampler kit from the *Radio Times* – and finished it; I've joined a choir; I've set up a bird table in the garden which I replenish regularly, and I keep a pair of binoculars and birdbook handy to identify what my parents' generation would describe as 'my winter visitors'; when going on holiday I start to pack a week in advance, and I've recently started to call my son by the name of my father, my partner by the name of my son and so on. At my last birthday I couldn't remember how old I was and had to work it out with a calculator. The crunch came when I found myself, in a fit of truly elderly good sense, deciding one day that the traffic was too heavy in town and that I should take the train instead. I thought I must be getting old when I packed a pair of flat shoes in my basket to wear while walking to the station. And I knew I was getting old when I forgot to wear them.

All the same, while the 'old' old age usually spelled more cantankerous and selfish behaviour, less tolerance of young people and views hardening along with the arteries, so far, speaking personally, the passing years (let's not call it age) have brought with them only improvements. (But then could anything have been worse than being young in the sixties?) Age has brought more confidence, knowing what one wants out of life, working twice as hard, getting good

153

at cooking at last, and having the courage Not to Put Up with Things.

When we say: 'I'm too old for camping holidays, too old for bed and breakfast, so old I can only cope with a four-star hotel' I think we're confident at last to say what we've always felt from the age of 10 upwards but just been too fearful to admit. And, when asked to a second-cousin-once-removed's first oboe recital in a modern church on the outskirts of London we're lying when we say, in a falsely quavering voice: 'I'm afraid I'm just too *old* for that kind of thing.'

While our grandparents may well have believed they really were too old, we of the sixties generation know that it's not really age that prevents us going; age is simply a kind excuse. It's really maturity that finally gives us the courage to refuse.

Garden China

RUTH RICHARDSON

Raised in a central London row of flats, with only the street in which to play, I've come to experience gardening only as an adult, and comparatively recently.

My parents' love of the wallflowers, geraniums and antirrhinums they planted in their home-made window-boxes – while certainly giving me a love of natural beauty, and some understanding of the seasons – somehow failed to fire me with the enthusiasm to become a gardener. I didn't fully appreciate the ductile potential of soil, the relative simplicity of sponsoring the natural growth of plants, nor the mystery and beauty of nature's multiplicity of form . . . until I moved in with a neglected garden.

At first, I made weeding forays, planted sunflowers and simple, rewarding annuals. But gradually, the garden called me. I found myself out there after writing a particularly demanding paragraph, or at the end of a chapter; tenderly training tendrils round trellis, providing splints for plants' tired limbs, or cutting long grass. Later I cleared patches, raked and sieved, landscaped on a large scale, levelled and seeded a fair-sized lawn, planted shrubs and trees, and learned to grow vegetables and fruits.

I began to recognise and cherish in others the same

155

creative and nurturing impulse, the same tender love of the natural world; in people of all ages and varieties, with whom I may have had nothing else in common, but this. I began for the first time to understand the appeal of the flower show and the prize vegetable.

The garden became important to my soul: a salve for the anxieties of writer's block, a source of sensual pleasure, and of spiritual replenishment after long stretches sitting at my work. I grew to appreciate in a new way how important those few plants must have been to my dear parents, raising our large family in a cramped slum flat several storeys above earth level.

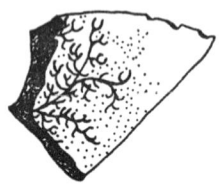

One of my especial delights, when landscaping or digging for spuds and horseradish, has been in turning up unexpected objects in the soil. Big stuff like lumps of brick from an old air-raid shelter and old bits of pram came first, but then, with sieving and raking I began to turn up more interesting things: squares of aluminium which neighbours told me were dropped by the Germans to confuse our radar in the Blitz, dogs' bones, clay pipes from lips long dead, glass marbles shiny with patina lost by children grown-up long ago.

Best of all has been the pleasure of finding broken crocks of china in the soil. The sharp eye, seeking the pale skin of a potato, or the rushing orange flash of a millipede, notices with some interest a little gleam of blue.

At first I'd lean over from my work to lay the new-found shard on top of my garden wall, so I could go on digging or raking. At first there weren't that many. Gradually, however, I seemed to be acquiring a collection, and a new discovery would cause me to leave my work for a few moments to add it to a growing pile, now garnered in a corner of the garden assigned for the purpose.

Rubbing off the dirt is always a revelation. Small bits of exquisite blue foliage or landscape emerge into the daylight after years underground. The detail on a smithereen somehow calls for closer attention than that on a whole piece of china. I find myself out there in my gardening clothes, hands browned and boots clogged with soil – puzzling out from what size dish my new old crock came, or how much of a repeat I have out of a repeating pattern.

There's a Thomas Hardy poem called 'Old Furniture' in which he talks about seeing:

. . . the hands of the generations
That owned each shiny familiar thing
In play on its knobs and indentations
And with its ancient fashioning
Still dallying:

Hands behind hands, growing paler and paler,
As in a mirror, a candle-flame
Shows images of itself, each frailer
As it recedes, though the eye may frame
Its shape the same . . .

The same kind of sensation affects me when I turn up a bit of china in my garden. I find myself thinking of the hands which shaped the ware, the hands which created the design, which laid on the transfer, and dipped it in the glaze – and the hands of those who used the dish: hands which washed and dried dinner plates below stairs and laid long-eaten meals upon them; imagined hands which dropped them, and dismayed, picked up and examined the pieces much as I.

Most of the hands I visualise are those of working women. I imagine this must be because of the sheer amount of domestic labour I know women have done, memories of my mother's household chores, and those of her own mother, an Edwardian maid-of-all-work. Possibly, too, as a result of a recent Arts Council film series about women in the Potteries, who in the 1920s and 1930s had worked as paintresses of Clarice Cliff and Susie Cooper ware. Brilliant designs which had been dormant in their hands for half a century were suddenly revived for the cameras. Observing the vivid facility with which the old shapes and colours flowed on to new blank ware from those working women's old worn hands was an experience which warmed my heart. It reaffirmed my belief in tactile memory and my faith in the untapped wells of human creativity in quite ordinary people.

My crocks serve as an emblem of what Wordsworth called the 'still, sad music of humanity' invested in every artefact – even in that rectangle of brown earth I call my garden.

The periodic resurrection of these remnants there reveals and reminds that others worked that patch of soil long before I did. Unearthing these fragments evokes a healthy feeling of time passing, generation following generation, of my own place in the procession, and of my own mortality.

As my collection grew, curiosity grew with it. What were all those gardeners *doing* with all those odd crocks? Thoughts began to emerge as from a budding urban archaeologist, and then theories about their provenance. My first conclusion, which was satisfying for a long time, was that they'd been tucked into the bottom of flower pots. When the plants over them had grown pot-bound and tenacious of their crocks, I thought, they were probably planted together outdoors.

One day, I decided my broken crocks deserved some real attention. I gathered them up, and took them indoors to the sink, where each battered and buried one of them was washed and laid out carefully to dry. Sitting with them at the kitchen table, I started to sort them out, dividing them up into little heaps by colour and trying to see if other characteristics might help.

The first thing I noticed during this process was the sheer variety of ware, and of design, my collection contained. There were thin bits and thick bits, chipped bits, and bits with clean breaks. There were pieces whose edges washed clean and others, more porous, whose crevices retained particles of soil. There were some whose background colour under the glaze was pure white, others were greyish or a drab cream. Glazes varied from translucent blueish-white to a soupy yellowish-grey, sometimes streaked with tiny rust-coloured crazing. On some the underglaze colouring was in black transfer, brown, or sea-green; some were hand-coloured, others embossed. There were pieces blotched in violet, dribbled in cream, and others traced with delicate wine-coloured arabesques.

The variety of blue shades was truly remarkable – from pale grays and the softest forget-me-nots, azures, aquamarines, ultramarines, and ceruleans to frank royal blues, cobalts, midnight blues, navy and blackish blues.

The multiplicity of designs made me despair of ever finding any which matched. Shards were covered with geometric patterns, stippled sepia patches, or the remains of hand-painted gilding on a soft royal blue. On some the transfer laid sharp and clear; on others the colour bled into the glaze, leaving a soft haze around the design. There were branches of deep purple foliage and light blue Asiatic pheasants, Grecian temples and snatches of English landscape so tiny that it was hard to imagine how they had ever been created.

The variety of these designs was entirely outdone by the ubiquity of willow-pattern ware. It was very easy to identify these pieces. Somehow even the smallest pieces seemed intimately familiar, as if I had absorbed with my National Health orange juice a knowledge and a secret love of this domestic manifestation of English orientalism. The largest pile of crocks – nearly half of my collection – was inscribed with some aspect of the tale, from the tips of the lovebirds' wings or the pagoda, to the catkins dangling in curious curves from diminutive willows. Its characteristic scaly, geometric borders called up vague memories of a half-understood story, involving the familiar figures on boat and bridge. The number of dishes represented by a fragment in my collection was manifest from the varying blues, thicknesses of ware and hues of clay upon which the design had been laid.

Among my still growing collection of odd bits of china have since been identified slivers of hand-painted eighteenth-century Chinese porcelain. The rest is British, cheapish Georgian and Victorian earthenware, decorated with blue-

and-white printed transfers. I've discovered all I can about
this sort of china. Blue was such a ubiquitous colour because
cobalt painted or transfer-printed under the glaze baked blue
in only one firing. And as for the history of willow pattern,
I found much to my surprise that, though the design dates
from the rage for chinoiserie in the late eighteenth century,
the legend associated with it was a Victorian invention.

None of the ware from my garden seems to have been
made much more than two hundred years ago. In archaeological terms, this is so recent as not really to register. Nine-
teenth- and even eighteenth-century objects hardly count as
noteworthy in most archaeological digs: sites in London, at
any rate, are excavated for Roman – or at the latest Elizabethan – rather than more recent remains.

What seemed most strange about my collection was that
so few of the pieces matched up. None could serve to recon-
struct an entire vessel like the pots one sees in museums,
laboriously reconstructed from much older finds than mine.
As the motley collection grew the thought began to form
that there were too many odd crocks for my 'gardener's
pots' theory to be the only credible one. Surely, if entire
plates had been broken, more pieces would marry?

While the history of blue-and-white transfer ware could
date them, it couldn't answer the riddle of my garden shards.
Yet their age nevertheless seemed remarkable when, after a
bit of research, I confirmed that my home was originally
built on land which was probably an open field until the
1870s. What had my part of Holloway been before my
garden was allotted to be a garden? The variety and number
of crocks might perhaps be explained if, like so many of
London's suburbs, the area had been market gardens: lots
of old crocks in lots of old flowerpots, perhaps?

But this idea puzzled me rather, as I recollected having

read Dickens's description in *Our Mutual Friend* of this district as the haunt of his character, the Golden Dustman, who made his fortune from owning rubbish heaps and paying women and children to sort and recycle their contents. Dickens described the district north of King's Cross as 'a tract of suburban Sahara'; a place where 'tiles and bricks were burnt, bones were boiled, carpets were beat, rubbish was shot, dogs were fought, and dust was heaped'.

A few days' work in my local history library convinced me that the land I now dig and plant with delphiniums and lupins lay just to the north of this 'suburban Sahara'. It was part of a large area known as Copenhagen Fields, crisscrossed with footpaths and hedges on old, old patterns, and pocked with Roman remains. The entire locality had long been grazed by myriad cows. Dr Johnson had once said – appropriately enough concerning relevance in history writing – that whoever came to write the history of the cow need not chronicle the number of cows milked at Islington. In the nineteenth century the same fields had provided a rendezvous for large political meetings, and a rural setting for family picnics, until the houses went up in the late 1870s.

None of this explained my crocks. But something I've learned both from gardening and writing history is patience. Like my blue-and-white china, things often emerge in the fullness of time. I let the subject rest while I finished a major piece of writing, continued with other projects and earned my living. Then, as can often happen in historical research, a possible explanation emerged when it was no longer actively being sought. During work in an entirely different context, I found a letter in a Victorian journal under the heading 'The Dusthole Nuisance', and signed 'ANTI DUSTMAN' in capital letters. It was from someone, living in Holloway, who despaired of ever receiving a regular dust collection, and who had decided to recycle almost everything, including broken china. Its writer revealed:

> The broken crockery (which is very considerable in my case) comes in very usefully when broken small, towards raising paths, or making new ones.

After reading this I tried to visualise this correspondent's hands alacritously smashing up broken china and laying down paths in my garden, or some neighbour adopting the same expedient, having read the letter or spoken to the writer over the garden wall. But there's something disturbing in the thought of intentional breakage of china, even in imagination, and I found it painful to visualise a hammer deliberately making my shards from larger ones. After a while the very same objection introduced itself which had caused me to doubt the flowerpot theory: if my crocks originated in one householder's purchases, why didn't more of them marry up? The idea that I was the present custodian of this correspondent's garden was finally rejected when I realised that the letter was written before my house was built.

The ensuing dejection didn't last long. A month or so later, a newspaper report caught my eye which almost caused me to disturb the quiet library in which I was working with a whoop of excitement. It surely provides the nearest thing to an explanation of my shards as I'm ever likely to find. The report concerned the exposure of an extensive fraud practised upon London builders by their delivery men, revealed at Marylebone County Court in the spring of 1854. The men had been sent out daily with horses and carts to purchase building materials. While they had charged their employers a standard rate, like all good entrepreneurs they had in fact bought them at a lower price and had kept the profit. The key point was the nature of the goods they had been sent to obtain: 'In the suburbs of London,' the journal explained, 'where so much building was going on at present, when it became necessary to found new roads . . . the builders found no materials so cheap or serviceable as broken crockery for the underpart. The depots for this material, it said, ' . . . were the various dustyards'.

So, many gardens might yield up the same sort of collection as mine – either because they now occupy the site of an old dust-heap, or because salvaged crockery had been used as hard-core in local building. Now I can quite happily visualise, alongside the piles of sand, cement and London stock bricks, the pile of broken crocks which probably stood in my garden when the street was no more than a stretch of open ground marked out with stakes and string.

My shards probably derive from a mix of the three possibilities I've mulled over – some doubtless fell out of a labourer's shovel, or tumbled down the side of the builder's heap and got trodden into the soil during the mixing of Victorian foundations. Others may have been laid down like cockle shells, all in a row, as garden paths or in shapes to prettify Victorian rockeries; and some no doubt got out there coffined in the roots of ferns and hollyhocks and Canterbury bells.

Now, when I take tea in the garden on fine summer days, it seems only right for it to be served upon blue-and-white willow-pattern china. I feel at home in the knowledge that dishes break, and that broken crocks get buried. I love my shards, those already found and those yet to reveal themselves from my flowerbeds – like the sea giving up its dead. Though their precise individual derivation will remain unclear, I've learned to accept the uncertainty. After all, evidence of baked clay ware survives in the environs of most of the human settlements known to history.

Perhaps now I should start burying my own.

Impressions of Britain Today

NATASHA VITALIEV
(translated by Kate Figes)

I first came to Britain in May 1989 with my husband and 8-year-old son. This was the first time I had ever travelled abroad. We were invited to stay with friends.

I thought often about Britain, in the Soviet Union, before coming. We know that Britain is a great power and one of the most developed countries in the world. We hear much about the Royal Family, and Margaret Thatcher, who has become particularly popular recently after the transmission of a television interview with Soviet journalists. She showed herself to be clever, an astute politician, and a charming woman with excellent skills of oratory and a dignified way of extricating herself from difficult situations. I know that the majority of you will not agree with me but it is important for you to know that most people in the Soviet Union think this way. People think that it is thanks to Margaret Thatcher that Britain has reached such a high level of development and lowered inflation. She has laid down the fundamental basis for individual freedoms.

It is not surprising that my first impressions in Britain

should be of Margaret Thatcher. She is cursed everywhere. Whenever I mention her name the reply is offensive or rude. Television and newspapers compete with each other to be offensive to Margaret Thatcher. In one paper she was shown in her underclothes doing semi-indecent things. On television she is shown as a puppet hurling insults and abuse. And this was on national television! Just try doing that to Gorbachev in the Soviet Union!

My son saw a calendar in London's Soho showing Thatcher and her husband completely naked, in different poses for each month. I find this insulting. No one else in her position would be able to tolerate this. They would sue, win and live happily ever after on their settlement from the case. But Margaret Thatcher has a sound enough mind and a sufficient sense of humour to be able to cope – she simply doesn't notice. I don't think that the British like their Prime Minister to be insulted in this way.

One of our friends is a well-known English journalist and he believes I am wrong to feel that this behaviour is insulting to politicians. He says freedom of speech is a sign of true democracy with freedom of expression and that one must study it. Perhaps one day I will be able to laugh at political figures dressed in their underclothes, but while this is somewhat foreign to me it isn't anyway very funny.

I hope that I am not beginning to bore you and I want now to return to the very beginning of my visit, to the cross-channel ferry. The buses and cars driving on to the ferry seemed like toys. The ferry was huge on the outside and chic inside. It was so clean and quiet and it smelt nice. Everybody on the ferry seemed happy and talked quietly. It was even quiet in the bar. Two children aged about 1 and 3 played by themselves; where their parents were I don't know. A small 2-year-old boy went up to a ladder and tried to climb it. I was a little worried about him and so went a little closer. Who was he travelling with? His parents were nowhere to be seen. The independence of these children from such an early age struck me. Boats at home are attractive and clean too, but crowded and noisy. Parents shout at their children as they run about screaming and shouting. A completely different picture. But the most interesting thing about the ferry was the toilets. I have never seen such smart establishments. Everything shone with cleanliness. There was toilet paper, soap, an electrical point for shavers and towels. A huge mirror reflected my astonishment and above all this hung a faint smell of perfume. You are, of course, used to this and don't notice it, but if you saw the state of Soviet toilets, you might understand my enthusiasm. I will not even begin to describe what they are like for you are bound to stop reading in disgust. We are still living in the Stone Age so far as toilets are concerned.

And here we are in London and it is the international feel that strikes me first. People of all colours walk or drive about. This is wonderful and very healthy. I think this is a sign of a flourishing society. It's only in the last twenty years that black people have appeared in the Soviet Union and you rarely meet them.

We have many friends in Britain who are feminists and I am often asked by women and men here what I think about feminism. Usually I am uncertain of my answer but now I want to speak frankly. I don't understand it and I don't understand what the struggle is about. Many Soviet women would agree with me. It seems to me that women in Britain have equal rights with men; rights at work, or rest, and freedom of movement. A woman can have a child without being married, both in the moral and the material sense, which many women do by the way. Women are free and

169

equal in the sexual sense. A woman's career depends basically on her capabilities, and there are a whole range of examples which illustrate this. Many women want to outstrip men physically by taking up sports that are traditionally male such as boxing and football. A married woman whose husband is employed can think about how she wants to spend her time, whether she wants to work full-time, part-time or just for a few hours a week. She can stay at home with her children if she wants, which in my opinion is the most noble thing to do, although perhaps not the most appreciated or interesting option. She can publish two or three articles a year in one of your many newspapers and magazines and maintain her social status by saying that she's a journalist. Women have a whole range of domestic assistance available to them. Shops sell products from all over the world, and deciding what to eat every day seems to be a woman's greatest problem. If a woman wants to, she can pursue her chosen career and do interesting things after work, without worrying that school may have shut down and her children are running around goodness knows where, without having to travel on crowded public transport, cursing herself because she didn't manage to run to the shops, and queue for hours, and then there's nothing for dinner. (And then if she does manage to buy something after work, she must spend one to two hours preparing it without the help of modern technology.) For that is how it is for Soviet women. British women do, of course, have their own problems. On the Soviet television programme *London-Moscow*, a British, female audience was asked what problems they had together as a family. After a long pause one woman replied: 'Deciding how to spend the weekend.' I think this answer is significant, for if this is a problem then what does feminism possibly need to achieve? And what about the fact that nature (or perhaps God) created men and women differently? I just don't understand it at all.

In spite of my problems understanding British women's need for emancipation, I do like them very much indeed. They are always happy, well dressed in interesting clothes and smile a lot. I can't imagine meeting a British woman who doesn't smile. Being in a good mood makes everything easier. I know very little English but I've never had trouble finding my way around. Complete strangers take time to help me. They draw diagrams and if it's on their way they always take you to your destination. Sometimes they ask where I'm from and when I say the Soviet Union they smile and wish me a pleasant stay. It's OK to be a tourist in Britain!

I've noticed a lot of handicapped people on the London streets. They seem to have a good life. I saw a special tour organised for the handicapped. They had good wheel-chairs and access to special toilets with adequate ramps. People help them on the streets. I remember seeing a woman helping three invalids in the park; two of them were in wheel-chairs. One day my husband was in a taxi during the lunch hour and there was a lot of traffic. Suddenly the traffic came to a complete standstill. At first he wasn't sure what had happened and then was surprised to see a blind woman with her guide dog crossing the road. This is not a surprising sight for you but it profoundly impressed the both of us. People take care of the handicapped here. We have handicapped people in the Soviet Union too, of course we do, but you never see them. They are not cared for, and they do not have wheel-chairs, so they cannot leave their homes. It is only now under *glasnost*, with many young men returning wounded from Afghanistan, that helping handicapped people has become an issue.

The attitude towards handicapped people must be an indicator as to a society's development. Another indicator is the level of poverty and unemployment. Both poverty and unemployment seem to me to be concentrated in Britain's inner cities. I remember the first homeless person I saw. He was an old man with a beard (perhaps he wasn't so old), dressed in rags. He was pulling a cart with a few belongings in front of Westminster Abbey. At the entrance to one of London's tube stations homeless people sleep on the ground covered with anything they can find. I remember seeing an old man at the entrance to Madame Tussauds. His head and hands were trembling as he tried to sell some little wind-up toys for fifty pence. I also remember seeing a middle-aged woman who was neat but very poorly dressed, buying some chips from a Wimpy bar. There's no need for me to recount any more. You've seen more of this than I have. But as a visitor I've noticed what a sharp contrast these sights are to the magnificent architectural backdrop of London.

Another problem seems to be the enormous amount of dirt and rubbish. London is far worse than other British cities. Our British friends say that the local authorities are at fault, that they don't do enough street cleaning. Perhaps this is the case. It's difficult for me to judge. But I have noticed that Londoners do have an uncanny ability to drop their litter just a few steps away from one of London's many litter-boxes. The Underground is as dirty as the streets. I've only ever seen it through a haze of dust. It reminds me of some kind of ancient catacomb: everything is worn out and in ruins. It is surprising that the trains run at all. The London authorities appear not to care about the state of the Underground service: it works, so what more do you want?

The horrifying thought is that if that's what the outside looks like then what can possibly be going on in those parts of the Underground we can't see? I've been in London for nearly a year. Nothing has changed, except that perhaps it's got worse. The cost of a journey has gone up, the system for buying a ticket seems to me to be unwieldy, and in spite of the rise in prices the escalators never seem to work and you have to walk up the stairs in order to get out. It's not unusual to wait ten minutes between trains. Now I understand why Londoners hate the Underground system. They only travel by tube in case of emergency.

I'm very fond of the London crowds. They're colourful and cheerful; everyone pushes past each other to get on with their day. I'd never seen punks before I came to London and I like them very much. They have such a bright and unusual appearance which is completely unacceptable. If I was ten or fifteen years younger I would definitely become a punk. There are even special shops for punks. If Soviet kids could see this they would be so jealous.

There are many mad people on the streets of London. No one seems to notice them: you are apparently used to them. But are Londoners safe? People get used to so many things, even terrorism. I was in the Natural History Museum with my son (a wonderful museum, incidentally, packed with interesting things, the best museum I've ever visited) when suddenly there was an announcement. Something had happened. Museum workers were running about trying to gather the visitors together. The police arrived and quickly cleared the building. I still don't know what happened. There was nothing about it on the television or in the newspapers. Our friends say that it was most probably a bomb scare. Once I was standing on the tube station platform and there hadn't been a train for half an hour. They said that the train had been delayed by a safety check. Everybody remained calm and considered this normal. Has even this become acceptable?

I want to return once again to the streets of London and talk about the traffic. There are so many cars and such narrow streets that it must be very difficult for drivers to get about. Nevertheless everybody sticks to the highway code and lets others go first. Drivers let pedestrians cross and always seem to stop for children. We spent a lot of time waiting on the pavement before we understood this. Your double-decker buses and black taxis are very attractive. And the fact that my husband has been able to get a taxi or a mini-cab in ten or fifteen minutes is staggering. It's very hard to get a taxi in Moscow. Once, my husband spent a whole day on the telephone trying to order a taxi two weeks in advance to take him to the station: they were either permanently engaged or no one would answer. When he finally did manage to order a taxi it was forty minutes late, although I am happy to say that he did just make the train.

Now I want to turn to shopping, a subject which is very dear to me. In Britain it is impossible to tell what time of year it is by looking in the window of a fruit and vegetable shop, for there is so much to choose from. Fruit and vegetables from all over the world jostle tantalisingly for space. In the Soviet Union you will only find fruit in the shops when it is in season: that means once a year. Spring is a particularly bad time for fruit. It is rarely imported and then only in very small quantities. Any child will tell you that June smells of strawberries, July of blackcurrants and cherries, August and September of grapes, melon and watermelon, October of apples and the New Year of Mandarin oranges and frost. The first time I went into a supermarket

I just wanted to cry. To have such a choice is the stuff of dreams.

When it comes to clothes shopping both the British and Russians have problems, although obviously the problems are different. We have not enough and you have far too much. When you have so much to choose from it is difficult to find something that you actually need. Once again you have become so used to such an excess of goods around that there is no need to justify the purchase of something that you really want. You have enough of everything that you need – transport, rooms in hotels and places in restaurants. There are even enough trolleys at stations for carrying your luggage. There is enough of everything and that is why the British are basically happy.

One British characteristic particularly fascinates me and that is your ability to joke in difficult or dangerous situations. It's a very well-known characteristic, one that has been described by writers such as Jerome K. Jerome, and which still exists in modern life. For example, a tube stops in the middle of a tunnel. Instead of panicking or searching for an explanation, two men begin to make jokes about the crisis and soon everybody in the carriage is smiling.

The most interesting aspect of any country is its people: their habits, characteristics and behaviour. I'd like to tell you what I've noticed during my stay here in Britain. I do hope that none of you will lose your sense of humour while reading my observations.

So here we go . . .

No one visits anyone without having received an invitation several days before. You don't just drop in, drink a cup of tea, have a chat, or watch an interesting film. You don't even drop in on your neighbours when you need salt or a cup of milk. Weekend activities are planned at least two weeks in advance. We once made the mistake of ignoring this and invited friends to a party that evening. It was a memorable occasion: only two people showed up. This would never have happened in Moscow. It was our fault for not following the customs of the country we found ourselves in.

One day in August my husband was speaking on the phone in Moscow to a friend in London.

'I'm coming to London in February.'

'When exactly are you coming?'

'I don't know yet but I would think it will be at the beginning of the month.'

'OK, come to lunch on the second Saturday in February.'

But then I suppose that's not surprising, for the British, nothing is so sacrosanct as their lunch. It doesn't matter what else happens – floods, fire, revolution, the mortgage rate or the poll tax, nothing will spoil the 'lunch hour' for the British. These two hours are for enjoying oneself. It's as sacrosanct as mass in church on Sunday.

Once my husband was giving a lecture in one of Britain's universities. The subject-matter was fairly serious – 'The Soviet Union and *perestroika*'. After the lecture a well-dressed, middle-aged lady with the ubiquitous English smile turned to my husband.

'Is it true that there will be civil war in the Soviet Union?'

'That is, unfortunately, a scenario that cannot be ruled out,' my husband replied. 'In several areas it has already started.'

'How nice!' the lady exclaimed, 'and who will they fight with?'

'If it happens, everybody will be fighting each other, it's a terrible thing.'

'Oh, it's lovely!' The lady left, pleased with her conversation, and sat down next to her girlfriend.

After a similar lecture in a small town, we were talking with quite a distinguished man who knew most of the people living there. But we couldn't finish our conversation for the owner of the house in which we were staying said to this person: 'We're now going home to have lunch, but if you would like to carry on with your conversation do come after.'

There is an English saying – punctuality is the politeness of kings. And sometimes the British follow this saying. But if you are invited to dinner at 8 p.m. and show up at 9.30 p.m. that's fine.

Whenever I'm at a party I always know exactly what I'm going to be asked first:

'How long have you been here?' and 'For how long are you staying?'

If the answer to the first question cannot be heard then particularly close attention is paid to the answer of the second.

Whenever I give a child sweets I know exactly what his or her parents will say: 'Don't eat too many, it's bad for your teeth.'

During our travels I have been inside many British homes so I can truthfully say that in most British bathrooms it is virtually impossible to mix the hot and cold water in order to get a nice even temperature. Why should this be? It's hard to know. Perhaps the plumbing is old and it can't be fixed, or it can be fixed but it's too expensive, or perhaps the British just don't consider tiny things like this to be important. You can get hot water if you try hard enough after all.

I've also observed people's behaviour on trains as I've

travelled. People usually sit down on two seats, one for themselves and one for their things. As the train begins to fill up people wander through the carriages looking for two spare seats. It's only when it's really full that people begin to take their things off the seats in order to let those people standing sit down. The best way to get a seat is to ask whether a seat is free.

The attitude to queuing has always interested me. It isn't often that the British have to stand in a queue but when this happens, it's taken very seriously. Smiles disappear and conversations cease. People stand away from each other as if to demonstrate their independence. If someone tries to jump the queue, he will be given angry looks, perhaps even a few caustic words will be said. And if this smart alec ignores these words and dirty looks then defeat will await him at the front of the queue, for the girl behind the window will ignore all of his excuses. She will look straight through him as if he isn't there (an interesting skill of use to every woman – just in case – I would have thought). This poor, unfortunate fellow could lie down and die and he would still not get served. If I were conducting a tour around Britain I would begin by advising everybody to respect queues.

I will now take my leave and wish you all every happiness and a speedy resolution to all your problems.